State of the Church: 2002

By George Barna

Published by Issachar Resources
(A division of the Barna Research Group, Ltd.)
Ventura, California

State of the Church: 2002
Copyright © 2002 by George Barna

Published by Issachar Resources, a division of the Barna Research Group, Ltd., 5528 Everglades Street, Ventura, CA 93003. All rights reserved. No portion of this book may be reproduced, stored in a retrieval system or transmitted in any form or by any means - electronic, mechanical, photocopy, computer scan, recording or any other - except for brief quotations in printed reviews, without the prior written permission of the publisher or author.

All Scripture quotations in this book, except where noted otherwise, are from the Holy Bible: New International Version. Copyright © 1973, 1978, 1984 by International Bible Society. Used by permission of Zondervan Publishing House. All rights reserved.

Library of Congress Cataloging-in-Publication Data
Barna, George
State of the Church: 2002/ George Barna
ISBN 0-9671372-6-8
Printed in Canada

Table of Contents

Section	Page
Acknowledgments	5
Introduction	7

Section 1 – The Religious Practices of Americans

Chapter 1	Going to Church	13
Chapter 2	Reading the Bible	19
Chapter 3	Volunteering at a Church	23
Chapter 4	Prayer	25
Chapter 5	Involvement in Small Groups	29
Chapter 6	Attending Sunday School	33
Chapter 7	Personal Evangelism	37

Section 2 – The Religious Beliefs of Americans

Chapter 8	The Importance of Faith	43
Chapter 9	Commitment to Christianity	47
Chapter 10	Who Is God?	51
Chapter 11	Jesus: Sinner or Savior?	55
Chapter 12	Personal Commitment to Jesus	61
Chapter 13	Is Satan Real?	65
Chapter 14	The Bible's Accuracy	71
Chapter 15	Earning Salvation	77
Chapter 16	Responsibility to Evangelize	83

Section 3 – Other Measures of America's Faith

Chapter 17	Different Flavors of Christianity	89
Chapter 18	Teenagers and Their Faith	101
Chapter 19	Protestant Congregations	113

Section 4 – Charting the Course

Chapter 20	Challenges to the Church	123

Appendix	page
Research Methodology	135
Related Resources	137
About the Author	139
About the Barna Research Group, Ltd	141

Acknowledgments

Every book is a team effort and I need to acknowledge the team that enables me to produce such books. My sincere thanks go to the Barna team members : Jim Fernbaugh, Meg Flammang, Lynn Gravel, Cameron Hubiak, Pam Jacob, David Kinnaman, Jill Kinnaman, Carmen Moore, Dan Parcon, Celeste Rivera, Irene Castillo, and Kim Wilson.

Other members of my team live with me; my family is a source of motivation, instruction and blessing to me. My wife Nancy has been by my side in our ministry and research efforts from the beginning, filling in the cracks at every step in the process. My daughters, Samantha and Corban, continually provide the encouragement and love that make the early mornings, hectic days and late nights (and very early mornings) bearable. Every book I write requires the Barna girls to surrender me to my calling to write for the Church. Thank you, girls, for "being there" for me – and for the Church.

Last but never least I acknowledge and thank the Lord Himself for blessing me with the opportunities, abilities and resources to serve Him. In the end, it is all about Him; I pray that I might recede so that Jesus and His purposes might be elevated. May the Lord find a way to use this offering for His kingdom.

George Barna
May 2002

This book is dedicated to all of the pastors in the country who have devoted their life to serving God and His people with love, intelligence, integrity and diligence. May you someday rejoice in hearing the Lord say, "Well done, my good and faithful servant."

Introduction

Seeking to understand the faith of Americans is no small undertaking. It is somewhat like trying to define happiness or beauty – it is easier to identify when you experience it than to objectively describe what it is. Faith is a complex amalgam of ideas, emotions, experiences, and truths that seem incapable of being easily quantified or explained. Those of us who traffic in statistics and sociological measurement typically agree that there is not a single indicator or factor that describes a person's faith completely or accurately.

Consequently, it is helpful to rely upon a series of measures that cumulatively provide a more comprehensive and reliable understanding of how faith is integrated into people's lives. Indeed, those who have experienced a robust faith speak of the richness of its influence upon every fiber of their being, fortifying the notion that faith is a complicated, nuanced, multi-dimensional reality that must be explored from various angles.

In this book I will describe the findings from Barna Research studies over the past two decades – primarily focusing on data in the past decade – which relates to people's religious beliefs and practices. To convey what we have found, I will identify specific measures that we track every year and provide the current national standing in regard to that factor; how various types of people (i.e., population subgroups such as men and women) stand on the matter; and some historical context by comparing the current statistics to what we discovered in surveys in the past.

There are four sections in this book. The first encompasses the survey measures that examine people's religious practices. The seven practices that we track consistently enough to report upon include church attendance, Bible reading, volunteering at church, prayer, small group participation, Sunday school attendance, and personal evangelism.

The second section focuses upon the religious beliefs of Americans. Over the past two decades we have explored several dozen different beliefs and theological perspectives of people. This section will describe our findings related to nine queries that we regularly ask. Those address matters such as the importance of faith, commitment to Christianity and to Jesus Christ, beliefs about God, Satan and the Bible, and perspectives on eternal salvation.

The third section explores several broad-based aspects of America's faith. The opening chapter of that section outlines the nature of several divergent groups of Americans based upon their faith inclinations. One such group is evangelicals. They are defined differently in our research than anywhere else. These are people who describe themselves as Christian; say they are absolutely committed to Christianity; possess an orthodox view of God; believe that the Bible's teachings are totally accurate; contend that religious faith is very important in their life; firmly reject the idea that Jesus ever sinned; believe that Satan is real; say that salvation cannot be earned; have made a personal commitment to Christ that is important to them; and believe that they have eternal salvation assured because they have confessed their sins and accepted Christ as their savior.

The second group described in that chapter is non-evangelical born again Christians. They have made a personal commitment to Christ that is important to them and believe they have eternal salvation assured because of their confession of their sins and acceptance of Jesus as their savior, but they do not meet all of the other criteria that define evangelicals.

The third group is notional Christians – people who consider themselves to be Christians but do not meet the born again criteria. These individuals are the most numerous of all adults who adopt the "Christian" label.

In that same chapter is a description of some of the distinguishing attributes of Protestants and Catholics. The other pair of chapters in that section focus on the faith of teenagers and particulars regarding pastors and Protestant churches.

The closing section touches on some of the challenges faced by America in light of the portrait of faith provided, and a few potential strategies toward meeting those challenges.

In all cases, the information is based on the annual survey that we conduct among a nationwide random sample of adults. To retain a measure of consistency, the vast majority of the information is drawn from studies conducted during January and February of a given year. (On occasion I will make reference to a national survey conducted during a different time of the year, but those studies are based on the same data collection and sampling methods as used in the primary studies.) The sample sizes vary slightly from study to study, but the surveys of adults are no smaller than 1000 people and no larger than 1204 people age 18 or older living within the continental states. Samples of this magnitude allow us to estimate that the maximum sampling error associated with the national statistics would be plus or minus 3.2 percentage points 95 out of every 100 times such a survey is conducted. For more information about the methods used to generate the survey data, consult the Methodology section in the appendix of this book.

In most cases this book provides data tables that examine statistics from several specific years: 1991 and 1992 (the first two years of the last decade); 1996 and 1997 (a half-decade ago); and 2000, 2001 and 2002 (the first years of the new millennium). Many of the graphics will provide macro-level data for the item under examination for each year from 1991 through 2002. It is hoped that these reference points will provide a greater sense of context for interpreting the figures that are current.

Faith and spirituality are incredibly powerful influences in people's lives and in American culture. My hope is that you will emerge from reading this book better informed about faith in America and personally motivated to respond to the challenges raised.

Section 1

The Religious Practices of Americans

Chapter 1: Going to Church
Chapter 2: Reading the Bible
Chapter 3: Volunteering at a Church
Chapter 4: Praying to God
Chapter 5: Involvement in Small Groups
Chapter 6: Attending Sunday School
Chapter 7: Sharing the Faith

Chapter 1
Going to Church

Perhaps the most widely examined measure of America's spiritual temperature relates to church attendance. Although attendance is a poor indicator of the spiritual maturity of an individual or culture because it does not address the substance of one's faith or a person's commitment to spiritual maturation, the long-term tracking of attendance at worship services provides a general sense of people's spiritual involvement. The research data show several general patterns that relate to church-going in America.

Noteworthy Attendance Patterns

First, the proportion of people who attend a church service in a typical week does not change much from year to year. Slightly more than four out of ten adults (43%) were present at a church service during a typical week in 2002. During the past five years there has been minimal change in the annual assessment of church attendance in a typical week: the range during the 1997-2002 period has been only three percentage points (from a low of 40% to a high of 43%).

This relative stability is what made the attendance jump after September 11 terrorist attacks so noteworthy: the increase of some 20% immediately following the disaster was a startling break from the steady pattern that had been established. Within a few weeks of the attacks, however, the attendance levels returned to normal.

For a decade prior to the mid-Nineties church attendance had been on a bit of a roller-coaster ride. Owing to various social upheavals during the late Eighties through mid-Nineties, attendance levels were comparatively volatile. After peaking in the early 1990s, attendance dipped to unusually low levels in the mid-Nineties before returning to more typical levels seen since 1997.

A second observable pattern is that most Americans attend church services at some time throughout the year. Although Americans do not attend church as frequently as they did in the Sixties and before, nearly two-thirds of all adults attend at least once during any given 12-month period.

A third trend that emerges is that relatively few people attend church services every week. In total, less than one out of three adults attend church with such consistency. This is partially due to a noteworthy decline in regularity among Catholics. The explosion in the number and quality of lifestyle diversions, combined with the nationwide decline in acceptance of rules and absolutes, has diminished people's sense of commitment and spiritual urgency regarding worship participation.

Subgroup Differences

Sometimes, though, looking at national averages obscures the real story. Beneath the surface there may be significant flux in people's behavior, masked by a virtual canceling out of the changes undergone by different groups. Three relationships stand out as significantly impacting church attendance patterns.

Generational realities are important. Baby Busters have had the lowest levels of attendance for more than a decade – but also the most stable levels. For more than a decade

Percentage of Adults Who Attended a Church Service in the Past Seven Days

	1991	1992	1996	1997	2001	2002
All adults	49%	47%	37%	43%	42%	43%
Busters	35	36	34	33	35	36
Boomers	50	40	31	44	42	44
Elders	57	58	46	52	49	52
Men	42	43	28	37	36	39
Women	55	51	46	49	47	46
Catholic	59	54	39	48	48	46
Protestant	56	51	45	49	50	53
White	48	46	36	41	41	43
Black	53	52	43	58	43	53
Hispanic	54	47	50	40	43	38
Northeast	43	44	31	37	40	36
South	52	55	43	50	46	50
Midwest	55	44	40	42	42	44
West	46	40	33	41	37	38
Evangelicals	NA	NA	77	89	82	86
Non-evangelical born again	NA	NA	55	55	57	57
Non-born again	39	34	23	29	29	31

Source: Barna Research Group, Ventura, CA

about one-third of this segment, now in the 19-37 age bracket, has attended church services in a typical week. That degree of steadiness is in marked contrast to the volatility of the Baby Boomers, now in the 38 to 56-age range. Attendance by Boomers has dipped as low as 31% and risen to a high of 50% in the past decade, although it currently resides at 44%. Elders, a combination of the two generations that preceded the

Boomers, have also been somewhat variable in attendance, although they have always been more likely to attend in a given week than were people from either of the younger generations. Half of the Elders(52%) currently attend.

Denominational identification also impacts attendance patterns. The most noticeable shift has been among Catholics. Even before the child molestation scandals were reported in early 2002, church attendance had been in decline among American Catholics. While the Protestant attendance level in 2002 was just three percentage points below the average recorded in 1991, among Catholics the level dropped by 13 points during that same period.

Catholics have historically had higher attendance levels than have Protestants, often attributed to the fact that failure to attend church is a sin to Catholics, while it does not have that same stigma among most Protestants. Since the mid-Nineties, however, Protestants have had similar or higher attendance levels than Catholics. In 2002, 53% of Protestants attended church services in a typical week, compared to 46% of Catholics. At least some of this decline among Catholics is a result of the weakening bond between Hispanics and Catholicism in the U.S.

Keep in mind that Protestants outnumber Catholics in the United States by about a two-to-one margin. Currently 53% of adults align with a Protestant denomination and just under one-quarter are self-described Catholics.

Ethnic patterns differ markedly regarding church going. A decade ago, blacks and Hispanics were more likely to attend services than were whites. These days, blacks remain the most frequent church attenders while Hispanics have become the least likely. The Hispanic church experience is undergoing radical change, between a shift from predominantly Catholic adherence to more involvement with Protestant churches as well as less consistent attendance at Catholic Mass among those who remain affiliated with the Catholic Church.

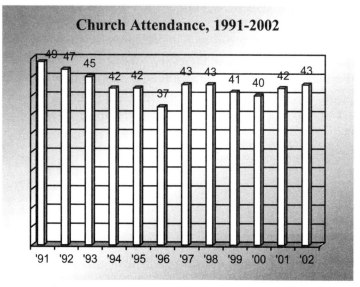

Source: Barna Research Group, Ventura, CA

It is also worth mentioning the massive distinction in attendance among different faith groups. Close to nine out of ten evangelicals attend church services in a typical week, compared to just less than six out of ten non-evangelical born again Christians, and less than half of the notional Christians (i.e., those who describe themselves as Christian but do not base their soul's eternal outcome solely on faith in Jesus Christ). Although the evangelical group is comparatively tiny – just 5% of the population – it is the segment that has set the pace in frequency of church attendance for many years. The most numerous segment – notional Christians – is also those whose commitment to Christ and to church involvement is least firm, if existent.

The Unchurched

Coinciding with the general decline in church attendance in a given week as well as in relation to the frequency of attendance by individuals, the current data show that the proportion of adults who can be considered to be unchurched has grown substantially since the early Nineties. In 1991, just 24% of all adults were unchurched; today, 34% fit that description. (We define people as unchurched if they have not attended a Christian church service during the past six months, other than for special events such as weddings or funerals.)

During the past 11 years the unchurched population has swelled thanks to increases in non-attendance among Baby Boomers (rising from 23% who were unchurched in 1991 to 31% today); women (jumping from 18% to 30%); Hispanics (19% in 1991 versus 33% in 2002); and residents of the Northeast (rising from 26% then to 38% now) and the West coast (up from 29% to 40%). Whereas the increase of unchurched adults in the West occurred during the mid-Nineties, there has been a slow expansion of unchurched people in the Northeast.

The data for Baby Boomers again shows evidence of fickleness in their church behavior. The attendance curve has moved up and down throughout the past decade as Boomers have struggled with meaning, purpose, priorities and theology during that time. It does not appear that the generation has come to a place of emotional, intellectual or spiritual stability yet; we expect to see continued inconsistency in the attendance pattern for Boomers over the next few years.

Chapter 2
Reading the Bible

Bibles are prolific in the United States. Although slightly more than four out of five adults consider themselves to be Christian, more than nine out of ten households owns at least one Bible. The big question, though, is what people do with the copies that they own.

Readership Levels

Reading the Bible was out of fashion in the mid-Nineties but has rebounded significantly since the onset of the late Nineties. After bottoming out in 1995 with less than one out of three adults (31%) reading the Bible during the week, other than during a church service, the figure has risen to its current high point of 42%.

This increase may well be the single, enduring benefit to emerge from the 9-11 terrorist attacks. During the 32 months prior to the attacks Bible reading had been vacillating between 32% and 39%, with a slow build in Bible reading beginning during the 2001 holiday season. While the 42% level was sustained through the Easter season of 2002, whether interest will again dip remains to be seen.

Who Reads the Bible?

As might be expected, the types of people most likely to read the Bible during the week are those in their sixties and beyond, women, adults who attend a Protestant church, blacks, and residents of the southern states. Evangelicals are three times as likely as individuals who are not born again to read the Bible in a given week: almost nine out of ten evangelicals read the Bible, compared to just one out of four non-born again adults. Six out of ten non-evangelical born again individuals read the Bible in a typical week.

Adult Bible Reading During the Week, Other Than at Church, 1993-2002

	1993	1996	1997	2000	2001	2002
All adults	34%	34%	36%	40%	37%	42%
Busters	27	28	27	32	29	33
Boomers	31	28	36	40	39	46
Elders	42	43	45	51	47	50
Men	28	29	34	35	32	37
Women	40	39	38	46	42	46
Catholic	22	21	24	25	25	27
Protestant	47	48	47	53	48	55
White	33	31	33	38	35	42
Black	40	49	58	63	52	61
Hispanic	33	45	47	33	32	33
Northeast	18	25	28	31	29	35
South	45	43	45	53	44	51
Midwest	38	31	30	35	37	38
West	32	34	37	35	34	40
Evangelicals	82	85	83	92	85	88
Non-evangelical born again	48	50	48	59	55	61
Non-born again	19	19	22	23	22	27

Source: Barna Research Group, Ventura, CA

In tracking Bible reading throughout the past decade, we find that Baby Boomers have had the least consistent involvement with Scripture, ranging from a low readership incidence of 28% in 1996 to the current high-water mark of 46%. That range of 18-percentage points exceeds the latitude exhibited among Baby Busters (a low of 21% in 1995 to a high of 33% currently, a 12-point swing) and among Seniors (from 39% in 1995 to 51% in 2000, a gap of 12 points). This inconsistency in Boomers' relationship with the Bible is indicative of the larger faith struggle that has defined their ongoing search for success, significance, security and serenity. That inconsistency is emphasized by the relative stability of Bible reading among the Baby Busters.

The three major ethnic groups in the U.S. – whites, Hispanics and blacks – have had very different history of Bible reading since 1993. Blacks have led the way every year during that ten-year period, rising from a low of 40% readership in 1993 to a high of 63% in 2000, before settling in at the current 61%. After some years of relatively low readership levels, Hispanics went on a Bible reading rampage during the mid-Nineties, but have reverted to the lower levels of readership since the beginning of the new millennium. After cresting at 47% readership in 1997, just 33% of Hispanics were reading the Bible during a typical week in 2002. Whites, due to the inconsistencies of Boomers, have had a jagged readership curve, dipping as low as 31% in 1996 and rising as high as the present-day 42%.

It is interesting to note that even though the Northeast remains the region with the fewest Bible readers, the proportion of adults in the Northeast who read the Bible in a given week has doubled since 1993! There have been small gains in readership in the South and West, while the Midwest has rebounded from a substantial decline experienced in the mid-Nineties to return to its higher levels recorded at the start of the Nineties.

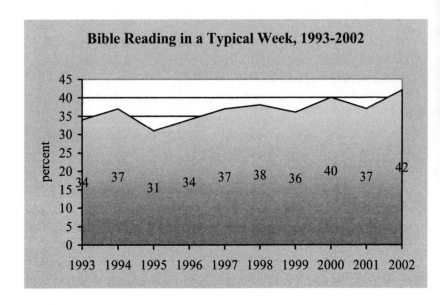

Source: Barna Research Group, Ventura, CA

One of the most encouraging trends is the significant increase in Bible reading among the non-evangelical born again Christians. While less than half of this segment typically read God's Word in any given week throughout the mid-Nineties, six out of ten of these adults had done so in the early weeks of 2002.

Chapter 3
Volunteering At A Church

One of the aspects of church life that does not change much over time is the number of people who volunteer their time to help out the church's ministry. In 1991, we found that 27% of all adults had devoted some time to assisting their church during the prior week. In 2002, the figure was 24% - a statistically significant difference, but for all practical purposes about the same number of people (given the combination of the small percentage decrease and the large aggregate population increase that has occurred during the past 11 years).

For the first time in half a decade nearly as high of a percentage of Baby Busters as Baby Boomers donated their time and energy to church endeavors in a typical week. For the past three years, Boomers were twice as likely as Busters to volunteer at a church. This year, however, the two groups were in a statistical dead heat regarding service involvement. As usual, people from the older generations were more likely than their juniors to assist in church activities.

A substantial jump in church volunteerism among Hispanics was responsible for the first significant increase in the Catholic Church in more than a decade. The long-term pattern of Protestants being more likely than Catholics to help out at their church persisted, though: three out of ten Protestants volunteered according to the 2002 data, compared to two out of ten Catholics. The gap between the two groups has closed somewhat, from a chasm of 16-percentage points in 1991 to just eight points today.

A related insight is that men are more likely to volunteer in Catholic churches, whereas women are the dominant volunteers in Protestant churches.

Evangelicals are twice as likely as non-evangelical born again adults to volunteer, and more than three times as likely as Notional Christians to help out at church in a given week.

Church Volunteerism in a Typical Week, 1991-2002

	1991	1992	1996	1997	2000	2001	2002
All adults	27%	24%	21%	24%	21%	20%	24%
Busters	10	13	16	17	11	12	22
Boomers	28	22	20	24	23	25	24
Elders	34	31	24	29	28	24	28
Men	24	23	17	20	18	19	23
Women	29	25	24	27	24	21	25
Catholic	19	16	16	19	15	15	21
Protestant	35	28	27	30	28	26	29
White	26	23	20	23	21	19	23
Black	38	31	29	29	27	27	34
Hispanic	22	23	32	23	19	17	25
Northeast	23	22	19	20	16	18	21
South	31	29	23	29	27	24	25
Midwest	30	24	18	20	21	22	24
West	20	18	23	23	17	14	26
Evangelicals	NA	NA	53	54	48	43	60
Non-evangelical born again	NA	NA	31	33	27	31	32
Non-born again	19	18	11	14	13	11	17

Source: Barna Research Group, Ventura, CA

Chapter 4
Prayer

Perhaps the most common religious practice among Americans is prayer. In a typical week, four out of five Americans (81%) say they pray to God. This has changed little since the mid-Nineties.

The older a person is, the more likely they are to pray during the week. Notice that while three out of four Baby Busters pray during the week, the same is true among slightly more than eight out of ten Boomers and nine out of ten Elders. Likewise, women are more likely to pray than are men, 88% versus 74%.

Blacks are the ethnic group most likely to pray (92%), with little distinction between whites (82%) and Hispanics (79%).

Regionally, residents of the Northeast and West are least likely to pray (three-quarters do so) while people in the South and Midwest are most likely (86% in each region).

Of the three personal faith practices examined – i.e., reading the Bible other than at church, praying, and evangelizing – prayer is the only one for which the involvement levels of Catholics and Protestants are virtually identical.

Evangelicals almost universally pray each week: in four of the past five years, our surveys have shown that 100% of the evangelicals interviewed had prayed to God within the previous seven days. Almost as many of the non-evangelical born again adults pray (97%), while a smaller percentage of the non-born again population (70%) engages in prayer.

Prayer During a Typical Week, 1996-2002

	1996	1998	1999	2000	2001	2002
All adults	83%	80%	77%	83%	82%	81%
Busters	76	73	70	75	76	74
Boomers	82	86	80	85	84	84
Elders	89	85	84	89	86	89
Men	75	73	70	77	75	74
Women	90	86	85	89	88	88
Catholic	92	88	83	87	92	87
Protestant	90	87	86	91	88	91
White	81	78	76	82	80	82
Black	94	89	94	96	93	92
Hispanic	100	84	76	82	82	79
Northeast	82	77	71	78	76	76
South	86	86	82	89	86	86
Midwest	85	80	78	85	86	86
West	77	74	78	77	76	75
Evangelicals	99	100	99	100	100	100
Non-evangelical born again	94	94	94	98	95	97
Non-born again	75	91	66	73	72	70

Source: Barna Research Group, Ventura, CA

It is worth noting that this information only measures whether or not a person prayed at all during the past seven days. Other surveys we have conducted show that there are significant differences across categories when other aspects of prayer are measured, such as the frequency of prayer, the amount of time spent in prayer, confidence in the power of prayer, and the content of people's prayers. In general, we find that most people who pray do so at least once a day; the total amount of time spent in prayer per day is less than five minutes; the most common type of prayer is a brief "grace" before a meal; other prayer time is dominated by requests for things the individual would like to receive; and most people believe that prayer can affect one's life, although they tend not to feel assured that their prayer will be answered.

Chapter 5
Involvement in Small Groups

One of the most interesting phenomena in church dynamics is the apparent lack of growth in participation in small groups during the past decade. This is surprising because so many churches, especially the evangelical "megachurches," have placed so much emphasis upon small group involvement. Although the studies do suggest that a larger number of people are involved in small groups in large churches, the *proportion* of attenders who participate is not much different than in smaller churches.

Nationally, during an average week slightly less than one out of five adults (18%) participate in a small group that meets for Bible study, prayer or Christian fellowship, other than a Sunday school class or 12-step group. (These aggregations go by a variety of names: cell groups, community groups, care groups, Bible study groups, etc.) The participation statistic has not budged since 1995.

Who Participates?

Small groups are very much a process adopted by Protestant churches, which explains why Protestant adults are two and a half times more likely to be involved in a small group than are Catholics. Presently, one-quarter of all Protestants attend a small group in a typical week. One out of every ten Catholic adults does so.

Surprisingly, involvement is not affected by age, although the driving motivations for involvement vary by age. For instance, Busters are most attracted by the relational aspect of small groups. Boomers are more likely to be influenced by the potential for knowledge acquisition, cross-family interaction and personal image impact (i.e., seen as a leader, a spiritual person, etc.). Elders are often involved out of a sense of church loyalty as well as spiritual development.

Participation in a Small Group, In a Typical Week, 1996-2002

	1996	1997	2000	2001	2002
All adults	17%	18%	17%	16%	18%
Busters	13	11	13	14	17
Boomers	16	22	18	17	19
Elders	20	21	20	19	18
Men	14	17	13	13	17
Women	19	19	20	20	19
Catholic	7	14	7	9	10
Protestant	24	24	23	23	24
White	14	15	15	13	16
Black	31	35	32	30	33
Hispanic	32	26	16	17	17
Northeast	12	11	11	12	13
South	19	27	23	19	25
Midwest	14	13	17	18	18
West	22	17	13	15	13
Evangelicals	43	51	55	40	53
Non-evangelical born again	27	24	23	26	25
Non-born again	8	10	8	9	11

Source: Barna Research Group, Ltd.

Black adults are twice as likely to attend groups during a week as are either whites or Hispanics. This is partly explained by the fact that a large proportion of Hispanics and a significant slice of the white population are Catholic. When Protestants alone are examined, blacks are still more likely to be involved, but the gap is not as substantial. Among Protestants, whites are the ethnic group least likely to be involved in a small group.

Small groups are most prolific in the South and least common in the Northeast (where Catholicism is much stronger) and in the West (where individualism reigns).

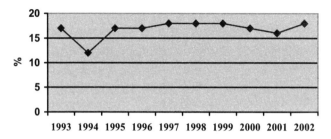

Adult Small Group Participation

Source: Barna Research Group, Ltd.

More than any other segment, evangelicals have embraced small groups. Half of the segment (53%) attends a small group during a typical week, which is double the proportion of non-evangelical born again adults who follow suit (25%), and nearly five times the percentage among people who are not born again (11%).

Chapter 6
Attending Sunday School

Adult Sunday school is one of the areas of personal spiritual involvement that has shown little movement over the past decade - until now. Between 2001 and 2002 there was a six-percentage point increase in attendance, rising from 19% to 25%. That is not only the largest one-year jump in attendance in more than a decade, but it also raised adult attendance to its highest level since the 1980s. What makes the increase even more impressive is that the national Sunday school figure had been stuck at 19% since the middle of 1998.

The research conducted does not provide direct insight as to why the increase occurred. Several congregational studies and various bits of anecdotal evidence suggest that the possibilities include a delayed reaction to the 9-11 terrorist attacks of the previous Fall, the heightened interest of young adults in specific Bible-related information that was available through Sunday school classes, and the rapid growth of Hispanics attending Protestant churches; the introduction of several new adult curricula that have gained a following, and a renewed emphasis by a handful of medium and large-sized denominations on Sunday school involvement. It seems likely that all of these explanations have contributed to Sunday school growth.

Demographic Explanations for the Rise

Baby Busters typically lag their elders when it comes to religious practices but they made up a lot of lost ground this past year with regard to Sunday school attendance. In nearly two decades of tracking this behavior, Busters have never reached the 20% participation level. They broke through that barrier this year, however, as one out of four Busters (24%) had attended a Sunday school class in the past week. For the first time in more than a decade, their involvement level was not statistically different from that of Boomers or Elders.

Adult Sunday School Attendance In A Typical Week, 1991-2002

	1991	1992	1996	1997	2000	2001	2002
All Adults	23%	22%	17%	23%	19%	19%	25%
Busters	17	10	13	18	14	14	24
Boomers	24	21	18	24	19	23	26
Elders	28	27	19	26	23	20	26
Men	21	18	15	22	14	16	22
Women	24	25	19	23	22	22	29
Catholic	8	9	5	14	10	3	14
Protestant	36	30	28	31	26	29	35
White	22	23	15	20	18	19	24
Black	31	22	32	34	29	29	40
Hispanic	30	18	18	32	15	11	26
Northeast	15	16	9	14	11	14	16
South	33	31	25	32	28	27	32
Midwest	20	19	16	19	16	17	25
West	18	18	15	21	13	15	25
Evangelicals	NA	NA	57	65	60	54	60
Non-evangelical born again	NA	NA	27	33	27	30	40
Non-born again	13	12	7	11	8	9	16

Source: Barna Research Group, Ventura, CA

Although a large gap remains between Protestants and Catholics regarding Sunday school – this is, after all, a distinctive of Protestant churches – there was an 11-point jump in Catholic involvement between January 2001 and January 2002. The key will be to ascertain whether or not that increase can be sustained since our tracking shows that smaller but noteworthy gains among Catholics in the past have not had staying power. This is not an insignificant matter since nearly 40% of the past year's growth in Sunday school attendance was attributable to Catholics.

Women maintained their dominance in Sunday school, an unbroken chain of two decades during which women have outnumbered men in Sunday school. The current gap between the genders – seven-percentage points – is on par with the average difference each year for the previous three years.

A substantial gap remains between blacks and non-blacks regarding Sunday school. Every year since the mid-Nineties there has been at least a 10-point difference between blacks and whites on this indicator, with blacks consistently reflecting the higher attendance level. The current gap of 16-percentage points is the largest measured since 1996. Interestingly, the current attendance levels of both blacks (40%) and whites (24%) are the highest either group has registered since the mid-Eighties.

Meanwhile, the proportion of Hispanic adults attending Sunday school more than doubled from 2001 to 2002. This is another point on the jagged curve of Hispanic involvement, which has ranged from a low of 11% in 2001 to a high of 32% in 1997. The current level (26%) is the highest mark recorded since 1997. Most intriguing in analyzing Hispanic Sunday school activity is the pattern showing a double-digit increase followed the succeeding year by a double-digit decrease. This three-year pattern of low-spike-low happened twice in the past decade. If the pattern holds true again, we will see a double-digit Sunday school attendance decline in 2003 among Hispanic adults.

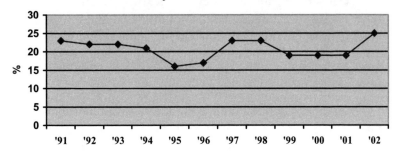

Source: Barna Research Group, Ventura, CA

There was no change in the past year among residents of the Northeast, small increases among people living in the South (up five points) and Midwest (up eight points), and a large increase among adults in the West (+10 points). Most of that increase, however, can be attributed to Hispanics.

Evangelicals remain the only segment among which more than four out of ten adults attend Sunday school. Six out of ten do so in any given week. Non-evangelical born again adults are about two-thirds as likely to attend as are their evangelical counterparts (40%). This reflects a 10-point increase from 2001 to 2002. A surprisingly robust 16% of the adults who are not born again attend Sunday school in a typical week.

Chapter 7
Personal Evangelism

Few religious practices generate as much anxiety as evangelism. Research we have conducted over the past decade consistently shows that many Christians acknowledge the importance of evangelism but have no heart or stomach for the process. In other words, millions of Christian adults affirm the importance of evangelism and want to see it done – by someone else.

While the reasons for such ambivalence or antipathy are varied – fear of rejection, fear of failure, lacking the spiritual gift of evangelism, lack of non-Christian friends, personal ignorance of Scripture, bad past experiences in evangelism, and so forth – the bottom line is that only half of the adults who have a grace-based relationship with Christ actually share their faith in Christ with a non-believer during the course of a typical year.

Involvement in sharing one's faith in Christ with non-believers has changed little during the past seven years. About four out of five evangelicals and roughly half of all non-evangelical born again Christians claim to have explained their religious beliefs within the past 12 months with someone who had different beliefs in the hope that they might accept Jesus Christ as their savior. (Note: because the intent of the question is to estimate how many people who have embraced Jesus Christ as their savior are actively encouraging others to do the same, we only ask this question of born again Christians – evangelical and non-evangelical.)

The demographic profile of evangelizers indicates that women are only slightly more likely than men to discuss their faith with non-Christians.

A massive gap in witnessing was evident between blacks and whites during the latter half of the Nineties. Blacks were much more likely to verbalize their faith to non-believers. The evangelism divide was at its biggest in 1997, when blacks were twice as likely as whites to share their faith. Things have changed since then, however, resulting in the virtual elimination of that gap during the past few years – primarily because fewer black adults share their faith these days. The percentage of born again blacks who have shared their faith with a non-believer at least once during the preceding year has declined by 38% since 1997. During that same time frame, the percentage of whites who engage in evangelism has not changed. Born again Hispanics are less likely than either blacks or whites to share their faith with non-Christians.

Incidence of Evangelism, 1996-2002

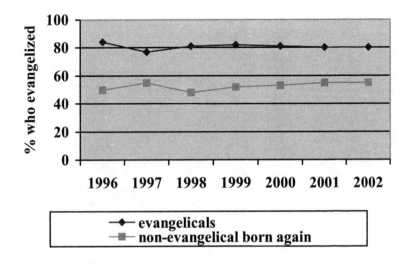

Source: Barna Research Group, Ventura, CA

Protestants remain considerably more likely to share their faith than are Catholics, but that gap is slowly narrowing, too. Data from the 2002 study show that during 2001, 60% of the born again (evangelical as well as non-evangelical) Protestants shared their faith in Christ with non-believers, compared to 48% of the born again (evangelical and non-evangelical) Catholics. That 12-point gap is a slight improvement over the 16-point gap that existed in 1996, when 54% of born again Protestants and 38% of born again Catholics had shared their faith with non-Christians.

One of the most striking outcomes is the evangelistic fervor of Baby Boomers. Once regarded as the scourge of the religious world, Boomers have matured into the primary evangelistic force in America. They are the generation with the largest total number of witnessing individuals as well as the generation that has the highest percentage of its members who share their faith with non-Christians. During the past two years Boomers shifted into overdrive evangelistically, outpacing their two elder generations (the Builders and Seniors) by a significant margin for the first time ever.

The region of the U.S. that has the fewest born again Christians – i.e., the Northeast – is also the region that has the lowest proportion of existing born again adults sharing their faith with other residents of that region. Although there are some observers who posit that matters have improved noticeably in the eleven northeastern states (and District of Columbia), the area still lags the rest of the nation in evangelistic boldness. In that sense, the Northeast has remained a kind of evangelistic self-fulfilling prophecy: there are fewer disciples of Christ in the region partly because there are fewer believers who are sharing their experience with Jesus among the non-believers they encounter.

The region with the greatest concentration of believers – the South – also has the highest proportion of believers who share their faith with non-Christians. The evangelistic profile of these two regions tempts one to adapt a well-known expression to describe this situation: the spiritually rich get richer while the evangelistically poor get poorer…

Section 2

The Religious Practices of Americans

Chapter 8: The Importance of Faith
Chapter 9: Commitment to Christianity
Chapter 10: Who Is God?
Chapter 11: Jesus: Sinner or Savior?
Chapter 12: Personal Commitment to Jesus
Chapter 13: Is Satan Real?
Chapter 14: The Bible's Accuracy
Chapter 15: Earning Salvation
Chapter 16: Responsibility to Evangelize

Note: Throughout this section evangelicals will be largely excluded from the discussion because their response to most of these items is the basis of how they were categorized as evangelicals. Two other groups of Christians – the non-evangelical born again and the notional Christians – will be discussed more frequently since there is variation in their responses to the items examined in this section. Each group is described in the Introduction of this book.

Chapter 8
The Importance of Faith

Social analysts often describe Americans as the most religious people on earth. While that may or may not be an accurate depiction, surveys have shown for many years that most American adults consider their religious faith to be a valuable, if not indispensable aspect of their life.

Two out of every three adults (66%) strongly agree that their "religious faith is very important" in their life today, and an additional 17% agree somewhat with that notion. This level of support for religious faith has remained unchanged for more than a decade.

Busters Don't Seem Overly Spiritual

One of the most perplexing findings is that Baby Busters are among the individuals who are least likely to claim that their religious faith is truly significant in their life. The media have made a big deal about the alleged spiritual focus and depth of the young adults, but the reality is that there is very little evidence of a substantial investment in spiritual matters. Their dismissal of religious faith as a defining attribute is a case in point.

A data pattern that is both significant and consistent over time is that the younger a person is, the less likely they are to portray religious faith as a very important element in their life. Although the gap has closed since the mid-Nineties, when adults in the Elders category were 22-percentage points more likely than were Busters to state that their faith is very important, the gap remains 14 points today. The closing of that gap is attributable to a rise in the percentage of Busters citing faith as significant (up four points) at the same time that the level among older adults has declined by a similarly minimal amount (down four points).

Adults Who Strongly Agree That Their Religious Faith Is Very Important in Their Life Today

	1996	1997	2000	2001	2002
All adults	67%	68%	67%	67%	66
Busters	56	57	56	56	60
Boomers	64	69	70	70	68
Elders	78	80	77	80	74
Men	59	62	62	59	58
Women	75	74	73	75	73
Catholic	65	64	65	66	66
Protestant	78	79	76	76	78
White	64	66	65	66	66
Black	85	87	89	83	76
Hispanic	71	63	64	59	67
Northeast	63	60	59	61	56
South	76	80	79	76	78
Midwest	65	65	63	67	65
West	61	62	62	61	59
Evangelicals	100	100	100	100	100
Non-evangelical born again	84	86	87	89	87
Non-born again	55	53	51	52	51

Source: Barna Research Group, Ventura, CA

Huge Distinctions

There are four other categories that reflect substantial differences among key constituencies. One of those is the distinction between men and women regarding the importance of their faith. Three-quarters of all women (73%) said faith is very important to them, compared to less than three out of five men (58%). This gap has remained unaltered for nearly a decade.

Protestants and Catholics also show both a large gap and a lack of change in that gap since 1996. Overall, 78% of Protestants and 66% of Catholics cite their religious faith as personally important. The gap is largely explained by ethnicity. Blacks, who are almost exclusively Christian, are 10 percentage points more likely than Hispanics, who are predominantly Catholic, to label their faith as very important.

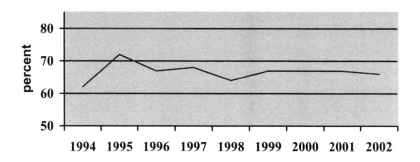

Strongly Agree: "Religious Faith Is Very Important in My Life Today"

Source: Barna Research Group, Ventura, CA

Residents of the Northeast and West were the least likely to proclaim their faith to be very important (56% and 59%, respectively), while the traditional esteem of faith among Southerners held fast (78% said it is "very important" to them). In examining the trend line since 1996 the sole region to experience any change is the Northeast, which has sustained a seven-point decline.

Soft Faith

It is worth noting that 13% of the non-evangelical born again adults stated that their religious faith is *not* "very important" in their life. While that is not a staggering figure, it does bring to light the fact that one out of every eight born again individuals admits that their faith is not a driving force in their life. Less surprising is the fact that half of all non-born again adults describe their faith as very important. If anything, the reality that half of the non-born again segment deems their faith very important, yet consistently ranks among the least spiritually involved people raises questions regarding their understanding of the potential power and significance of faith. At the same time, their description of such a limited faith as being very important underscores how difficult it will be to move them to embrace and pursue a more meaningful and life-shaping faith experience.

Chapter 9
Commitment to Christianity

If there is any single indictor that persuasively reflects the lukewarm nature of the faith of Americans who call themselves Christian – and even many of those who say they have turned their lives over to Jesus Christ – it is their description of their commitment to the Christian faith.

Currently, only half of the adults who say they are Christian contend that they are "absolutely committed" to the Christian faith. That number has remained firm since we began using it as a measure in 1996.

One of the most unnerving outcomes is how few Baby Busters claim to be absolutely committed to Christianity. Although the 2002 figure is the highest yet measured among the Busters (38%), it remains not only the lowest figure among any of the four adult generations but also substantially below the national norm. The fact that this condition is consistent with the low levels of spiritual investment among young adults may give greater credence to the reliability of the research, but raises disturbing possibilities regarding the future of the Christian faith in the U.S.

Typical Relationships

Given other data relationships that have consistently emerged over the past decade it was not surprising to discover that women are more committed to the Christian faith than are men, and that Protestants are more likely to indicate absolute commitment than are Catholics.

Percentage of Adults Who Say They Are Christian And Are "Absolutely Committed" to Christianity

	1996	1997	2000	2001	2002
All adults	44%	52%	49%	49%	50%
Busters	27	35	32	34	38
Boomers	43	52	50	52	54
Elders	47	54	54	54	50
Men	38	46	41	44	46
Women	49	57	55	54	54
Catholic	33	44	38	39	41
Protestant	51	56	53	53	53
White	44	52	50	51	53
Black	48	59	52	51	56
Hispanic	28	42	35	30	33
Northeast	36	43	39	40	40
South	51	58	59	58	55
Midwest	42	47	45	50	48
West	45	59	42	43	53
Evangelicals	95	93	97	88	86
Non-evangelical born again	52	63	65	68	63
Non-born again	30	36	27	28	35

Source: Barna Research Group, Ventura, CA

Similarly, the general faith patterns that describe Hispanics and people from the four geographic regions held true on this variable as well. Blacks and whites had similar levels of commitment to Christianity (56% and 53%, respectively) while Hispanics were substantially less likely to assert having such a commitment (33%). Regionally, just 40% of those who live in the Northeast claimed to be absolutely committed to Christianity, compared to 48% among folks in the Midwest and 55% among people living in the South. The aberration was the

53% of westerners who said they are absolutely committed to Christianity. That is likely a combination of two opposing factors. On the one hand our research notes that millions of people on the Left Coast simply have a less lofty notion of commitment, in general. On the other hand, we also find that among Christians in the West there is often a heightened intensity of commitment fueled by the greater opposition that Christians face amidst greater diversity and spiritual competition found in the West.

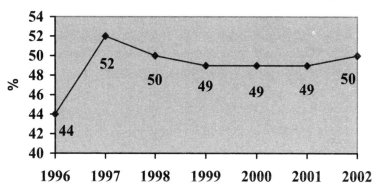

Source: Barna Research Group, Ventura, CA

Even You, Brother?

The data table on the preceding page points out that even evangelicals sometimes lack a total commitment to the cause of Christ. Fourteen percent of the evangelical base – that's one out of every seven evangelicals – admits to *not* being absolutely committed to Christianity. More than *one-third* of the non-evangelical born again segment offer the same admission. Two-thirds of those who do not claim to be assured of their salvation because of Christ's death and resurrection for them admit to not be absolutely devoted to the cause of Christ.

It is curious that as recently as 2000, some 97% of evangelicals claimed to be absolutely committed to Christianity, yet the number has plummeted to just 86% in 2002. An 11-point drop in just two years is significant in its own right. However, the fact that the decline in question relates to the level of faith commitment among the population segment that is typically most intensely loyal to Christ and most actively involved in their faith could well be a sign that the strength of the evangelical community is dissipating. The next two years will provide greater clarity to this unattractive possibility.

Chapter 10
Who Is God?

Almost everyone in America believes in some kind of deity or higher power. However, survey results showing that more than nine out of ten adults "believe in God" may be deceiving once you realize that a large proportion of those people believe in a god or gods other than the God of Israel.

About seven out of ten adults believe in a God who is the "all-powerful, all-knowing, perfect creator of the universe who rules the world today." The percentage shifts by a point or two each year, but there has been remarkable consistency in this figure since the mid-Eighties. For a while it was believed that "new age" concepts of deity would seduce the public, but that has turned out not to be the case. Descriptions of unbiblical deities have not caught on very quickly.

Who – or what – are the pretenders to God's throne? In 2002, just 8% defined God as the "total realization of all human potential," another 8% described God as "a state of higher consciousness that a person might reach," and 3% each said that "there are many different gods, each with a different authority and power" or that "everyone is God." Only 4% outright reject the existence of God, regardless of definition. (In fact, agnostics outnumber atheists by better than a 3:1 margin.)

Percentage of Adults Who Believe in God as Described in the Bible

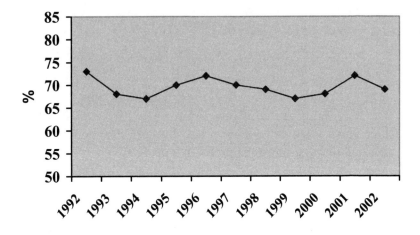

Source: Barna Research Group, Ventura, CA

Patterns

As might be expected, the younger an adult is, the more likely they are to embrace a non-biblical understanding of God. Similarly, men are more likely than women to embrace a notion of God other than that defined in Scripture; Catholics are more likely than Protestants to embrace an unorthodox view of God; and people living in the West and Northeast are less likely to buy into the God of Israel than are people in the South and Midwest.

One surprise was that Hispanics emerged as the segment most likely to endorse an orthodox biblical perception of God. Seventy-nine percent of Hispanics did so, compared to a slightly lower percentage of blacks (75%) and a lower proportion of whites (68%).

Percentage of Adults Who Describe God as the All-Powerful, All-Knowing Perfect Creator of the Universe Who Rules the World Today

	1992	1996	1997	2000	2001	2002
All adults	73%	72%	70%	68%	72%	69%
Busters	64	71	70	63	69	64
Boomers	68	73	69	70	73	70
Elders	83	73	71	72	75	75
Men	68	70	66	63	69	65
Women	78	75	72	73	75	72
Catholic	71	76	74	65	72	70
Protestant	83	81	77	80	82	79
White	73	70	67	66	69	68
Black	81	83	78	84	84	75
Hispanic	64	84	92	73	78	79
Northeast	66	73	64	57	66	56
South	82	76	77	79	79	79
Midwest	72	77	69	67	72	73
West	69	61	64	62	66	60
Evangelicals	NA	100	100	100	100	100
Non-evangelical born again	NA	91	90	88	93	90
Non-born again	60	59	53	52	56	54

Source: Barna Research Group, Ventura, CA

Whereas evangelicals, by definition, believe in a biblical view of God, and 90% of the non-evangelical born again believers do so, only six out of ten Notional Christians adopt a Bible-based understanding of the nature and person of God.

God and Politics

It may not be polite to mix politics and religion in polite conversation, but the research finds that there are some fairly strong correlations between political leanings and views of God.

For instance, Republicans are significantly more likely than Democrats to possess a biblical definition of God (82% compared to 70%). The most amazing outcome, though, is just how independent those who are Independent voters really are: only half of the Independents (55%) believe in the God portrayed in Scripture.

A similar pattern was found regarding political ideology. Eighty-three percent of those who say they are mostly conservative on sociopolitical matters had a biblical view of God. That was nearly double the proportion of self-defined liberals (47%) who held such a God-view.

Chapter 11
Jesus: Sinner or Savior?

Jesus Christ has always been a controversial figure. This is neither news nor surprising: anyone who is described as the sole savior of all humanity is bound to set off arguments. What may be unexpected, however, is the extent to which modern-day people disagree about the character of Jesus. Such debate is odd because the only way of understanding His nature and character is by relying upon written documentation – in this case, the Bible.

What may be most amazing, however, is that so many people who are committed to the Christian faith and who believe that the Bible is an accurate document conclude that Jesus was a sinner. While there is no biblical evidence to support that contention – in fact, the Bible is clear that Jesus was sinless – millions of Christians declare Him to be just like the rest of us when it comes to temptation – fallen, guilty, impure- If that point of view is to be taken seriously, the endpoint would be the same as for the rest of us, too – that is, Jesus is in need of a savior!

Little Change

Americans have not changed their views on the sin nature of Jesus during the eight years Barna Research has been measuring this quality. While there have been very minor fluctuations in opinion from year to year, the differences have not been large enough to reach the point of statistical significance.

If we aggregate the data by removing the measures of intensity (i.e., the "strongly" and "somewhat" delineations), Americans are about evenly split as to whether or not Jesus sinned. As the table below shows, the national survey in 2002 found that 25% strongly agree that Jesus Christ sinned while on earth and another 19% agreed somewhat with that sentiment. Just 8% disagreed somewhat while 40% strongly disagreed with that characterization. The remaining 8% were not sure what to think. If we compare the "agree" and "disagree" opinions, it is a 44% to 48% split. If, however, we recognize that only those individuals who said they "strongly disagree" with the contention unequivocally accept the divinity of Christ, then the figures portray 40% accepting the purity of Christ versus 52% who believe He did or may have sinned.

"When He Lived on Earth, Jesus Christ Committed Sins…"

	1996	1998	2000	2002
Strongly agree	22%	24%	20%	25%
Somewhat agree	20	19	19	19
Somewhat disagree	11	8	9	8
Strongly disagree	37	41	43	40
Don't know	10	9	9	8

Source: Barna Research Group, Ventura, CA

Notice that this is a theological issue on which relatively few people – less than one out of every ten – profess to ignorance. More than nine out of ten adults have an opinion on this matter – and, in nearly two out of three cases, people hold very intense opinions on the subject.

Who Stands Where?

Following the consistent pattern, the youngest adults are those most likely to contend that Jesus was a sinner. Catholics are slightly more likely than Protestants to hold that view. There were no differences based upon gender, ethnicity, region of residence, education, income, or marital status. There was a significant distinction between those who attend mainline Protestant churches and those attending non-mainline congregations: the former were more likely to strongly affirm the belief that Jesus was a sinner (29% versus 21%, respectively).

At the opposite end of the continuum – i.e., strong disagreement with the notion that Jesus sinned – are relatively larger proportions of married people (46% compared to 32% of the not married segment, including just 24% of those who have never been married), born again adults (60% of the non-evangelical born agains vs. 28% of the Notional Christians and 16% of atheists), and those who attend non-mainline Protestant churches (53% compared to 35% of the mainline and 32% of Catholic adherents).

Political leanings were correlated to views on Christ's nature. Party affiliation reflected some large differences: a majority of Republicans adamantly rejected the notion that Jesus sinned (53%) while less than half of the registered Democrats (40%) and Independents (32%) concurred. Ideological leanings also related to this issue. Conservatives were nearly twice as likely as those who said they are middle-of-the-road, and three times as likely as self-described liberals to firmly reject the idea that Jesus sinned.

Adults Who Strongly Disagree That When Jesus Christ Was On Earth He Committed Sins

	1996	1997	2000	2001	2002
All adults	37%	42%	43%	41%	40%
Busters	29	28	34	34	34
Boomers	36	45	46	43	41
Elders	44	52	51	45	46
Men	36	40	42	38	39
Women	38	44	45	43	41
Catholic	31	36	34	33	32
Protestant	48	51	53	50	48
White	36	40	42	41	41
Black	46	56	61	43	47
Hispanic	41	50	39	37	32
Northeast	30	34	30	34	32
South	45	50	41	47	47
Midwest	37	37	56	40	36
West	35	46	41	38	40
Evangelicals	100	100	100	100	100
Non-evangelical born again	50	54	60	54	54
Non-born again	23	62	26	26	27

Source: Barna Research Group, Ventura, CA

Born Again Confusion

Perhaps the most shocking revelation is that such a large number of non-evangelical born again Christians believe that Jesus sinned. One out of five strongly agree that He sinned, an additional one out of eight agreed less vehemently, and 6% disagreed somewhat, with 5% more not sure what to believe. In other words, nearly half of the non-evangelical born again segment (46%) did not strongly disagree with the notion that Christ sinned.

Granted, the non-evangelical born again population far outpaced other adults in terms of rejecting the Jesus-as-sinner view. Yet, the fact that almost half of the group relies upon an imperfect, guilt-ridden, savior who apparently possesses limited power is quite remarkable.

How Non-Evangelical Born Again Christians Respond to the Notion That Jesus Sinned

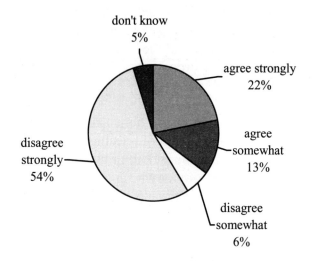

Source: Barna Research Group, Ventura, CA

Chapter 12
A Personal Commitment to Jesus Christ

Most Americans believe that they have made a personal commitment to Jesus Christ that is still important in their life these days. Currently, about two-thirds of all adults contend they have such a commitment in place. That figure has remained stable for more than a decade. In fact, I first used this question in a nationwide survey in 1982 – a full two decades ago – and there has been virtually no change in the percentage during that period. In 1982, 60% said they had made a personal commitment to Jesus that was still important to them; the current figure is 65%.

What Types of People Say They Are "Personally Committed?"

It is useful to mention that a majority of virtually every demographic segment we studied said they had made such a commitment to Christ. Among the few exceptions were adults who are not born again (41% of whom say they have made a commitment); adults who have never been married (47%); atheists and agnostics; unchurched adults (34%); and political liberals (43%).

Looking more closely at differences in the remaining five dozen subgroups we examined, we find that women are more likely than men to make such a commitment; Baby Boomers are the most likely to do so and Baby Busters the least likely, with the Elder generation in-between; married adults are more likely than single adults (70% compared to 57%, respectively); and blacks are the ethnic group most likely to do so, while Hispanics are the least likely.

Four out of five Protestant adults have made a personal commitment to Christ, compared to just half of all Catholics. Some analysts have posited that this may be an issue of language and conceptualization more than a real difference in religious practice, suggesting that the "personal commitment" terminology is born out of the Protestant world and may have no immediate meaning to a Catholic. While that may have been true in the 1980s, this explanation is not as appealing these days due to the homogenization of religious language and the closer ties between Protestant and Catholic churches.

There are still huge regional differences regarding a commitment to Christ. Adults in the Northeast are the least likely to claim such a tie, followed closely by people in the West, with Midwesterners more likely to have a commitment and Southerners by far the most likely of all. The percentage of Northeastern adults who claim a personal commitment to Jesus was exactly the same in 2002 as it was in 1982. Geographically, we discovered that the largest states in the nation have vastly divergent rankings on this matter. For instance, California and New York were among the states with the fewest adults who had made a personal commitment (50% and 49%, respectively), while Texas was one of the highest in the nation (86%). Other large states, like Florida (70%) and Illinois (62%) were closer to the national norm.

Political ideology is also related to having made such a commitment. Republicans far outdistance either Democrats or Independents on this matter (80% versus 66% and 55%, respectively). In like manner, conservatives (81% of whom have made a personal commitment) are clearly distinguished from moderates (62%) and liberals (43%).

Adults Who Say They Have Made A Personal Commitment to Jesus Christ That Is Important In Their Life Today

	1982	1991	1992	1996	1997	2000	2001	2002
All adults	60%	62%	65%	64%	68%	66%	66%	65%
Busters	N/A	48	51	57	64	57	60	56
Boomers	56	66	69	66	69	70	70	72
Elders	64	66	69	68	70	73	70	66
Men	55	56	57	60	63	61	62	59
Women	64	67	71	69	72	72	70	69
Catholic	N/A	53	52	58	62	59	62	54
Protestant	N/A	78	80	78	81	82	80	81
White	N/A	60	66	63	68	66	67	66
Black	N/A	76	75	77	87	85	73	75
Hispanic	N/A	71	53	77	53	58	60	56
Northeast	51	51	53	55	56	52	53	52
South	69	70	76	75	77	78	75	77
Midwest	63	62	68	68	70	68	66	65
West	52	60	56	55	63	61	66	58
Non-born Again	44	41	41	42	43	43	43	41

Source: Barna Research Group, Ventura, CA

It is quite astounding that although Protestant and Catholic churches have raised – and spent – close to one-trillion dollars on domestic ministry during the past two decades, there has been no measurable increase in one of the expressed purposes of the church: to lead people to Christ and have them commit their lives to Him.

Chapter 13
Is Satan Real?

It is not surprising that research highlights numerous examples of theological inconsistencies to which people cling. After all, Americans spend relatively little time reading the Bible, most of us think that we already know what the Bible has to say (and, therefore, we are not open to new information or perspectives), and the average church-goer gleans relatively little theological insight from the church services attended.

If we ever needed evidence of the biblical illiteracy of Americans, the fact that nearly half contend that Jesus sinned would be a great starting point. But that case would be strengthened by recognizing that even greater numbers of Americans – including a majority of those who are born again Christians – do not believe that Satan is real.

Dissin' the Devil

Presently, six out of ten adults agree "Satan is not a living being but is a symbol of evil." Two-thirds of those adults hold firmly to that contention. Just one out of four adults argue strongly that Satan is more than symbolic.

The figures in the accompanying table show that Americans have a rather fixed view of Satan. This deception regarding Satan's existence is, of course, one of the pivotal strategies in the spiritual battle facing America today. After all, you cannot win a battle – and would not even try to win – if you don't believe your enemy exists or that the enemy is to be taken seriously.

"The Devil (Or Satan) Is Not A Living Being But Is Just A Symbol of Evil"

	1994	1996	1998	2000	2002
Strongly agree	36%	39%	42%	40%	42%
Somewhat agree	23	21	19	18	19
Somewhat disagree	12	9	8	9	8
Strongly disagree	22	25	25	27	24
Don't know	7	7	7	7	7

Source: Barna Research Group, Ventura, CA

Surprisingly, the older a person is, the more likely they are to strongly affirm that Satan is symbolic. While one might expect the younger crowd to write of the Devil as fantasy, it appears that younger adults are more prone to accept the possibility of a supernatural evil force. About one-third of the Baby Busters strongly agree that Satan is symbolic compared to half of the Elders (i.e., people 57 or older). Busters are not convinced that such a dark force exists but reserve the right to believe that it may.

Catholics consistently outnumber Protestant when it comes to accepting the Satan-as-symbol philosophy. While the Catholic leanings of many Hispanics explain the high proportion of Latinos who dismiss the devil, the fact that blacks are the most likely ethnic group of all to reject the existence of Satan is unexpected. A majority of blacks (59%) strongly agree that Satan is biblical symbolism, a concept embraced by less than four out of ten whites (38%). Overall, nearly three-quarters of all black adults agree, either strongly or somewhat, that Satan is not real.

Adults Who Strongly Agree That "The Devil, or Satan, Is Not A Living Being But Is Just A Symbol of Evil"

	1991	1996	1997	2000	2001	2002
All adults	35%	39%	42%	40%	39%	42%
Busters	33	32	37	41	35	37
Boomers	32	39	41	36	39	42
Elders	38	44	47	47	47	51
Men	33	37	38	37	38	36
Women	37	41	46	43	41	48
Catholic	39	46	49	52	45	52
Protestant	34	39	42	41	38	43
White	33	38	41	38	38	38
Black	41	53	47	47	51	59
Hispanic	44	55	45	49	37	51
Northeast	39	41	42	39	39	44
South	32	40	41	44	41	48
Midwest	36	38	45	41	38	35
West	33	38	40	36	40	39
Non-evangelical born again	NA	46	47	45	42	47
Not born again	36	41	44	43	41	43

Source: Barna Research Group, Ventura, CA

The firm belief that Satan exists is fairly evenly distributed across the various subgroups of our population. There are a few groups – such as Catholics (11%), blacks (15%), liberals (16%) and Notional Christians (15%) who are slightly less likely to strongly affirm Satan. The handful of groups that have the greatest concentration of adults who expressed certainty about the devil's existence included conservatives (39%) and people who are most active in their faith (41%). Interestingly, born again Christians were no more likely to firmly believe in Satan than were adherents of non-Christians faiths (primarily Judaism and Islam). In fact, adherents of non-Christian faiths were somewhat less likely than were born again believers to firmly reject the reality of Satan.

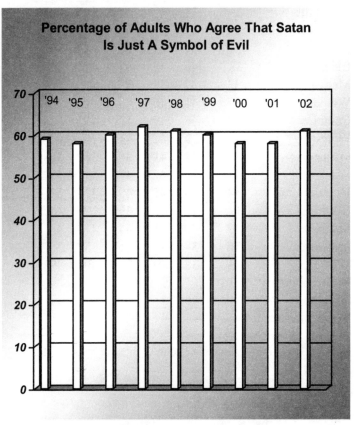

Source: Barna Research Group, Ventura, CA

Born Agains No Different

A powerful illustration of the theological weakness of the born again community is the finding that a majority of born again adults do not believe that Satan is real. About half of these people (47%) strongly affirm that Satan is symbolic, plus another 15% who offer moderate agreement to this idea. That's nearly two out of every three born again Christians promoting the notion that the Bible's content about God's enemy is not to be taken seriously. It should be pointed out that this condition has been in place for many years; this is not a recent theological phenomenon.

Just as the erroneous views on the sinless nature of Jesus undermines the power of the argument regarding a need for a savior, so does the dismissal of a real enemy weaken the exhortation from born again adults to accept Christ as one's savior. Are we to be saved by a sinner who apparently is incapable of resisting temptation? And what or who are we to be saved from? These are reasonable questions that flow quite naturally from the inconsistent doctrinal positions of tens of millions born again adults.

Variability Is Evident

An intriguing sidelight to this discussion is that unlike many other belief statements that we track each year, there is some degree of variability evident in the data regarding Satan's existence. This indecision is particularly noticeable among several subgroups: Hispanics, Catholics and blacks.

Chapter 14
The Bible's Accuracy

The Christian faith is not based on oral tradition alone. The core doctrine of the faith is drawn from its foundational document, the Bible. We know that the Bible remains the best-selling book of all-time, and continues to sell millions of copies in the U.S. ever year. There are more than 1500 different versions, translations and editions of the Bible available for purchase in the U.S. More than nine out of ten Americans own at least one copy of the Bible. About six out of ten adults read from the Bible sometime during the course of the year. Statistics such as these intimate that we have adopted the Bible as a loved and accepted text – an ancient text that remains relevant to our lives nearly two thousand years after it was written.

But how we treat the content of the Bible is a different matter. Less than half of all adults (46%) are strongly persuaded that the Bible is totally accurate in all of its teachings. Combining that group with those who are somewhat confident of the Bible's accuracy (17%), the proportion swells to almost two-thirds of the adult population (63%). The one-third who contends that the Bible is not completely accurate in its teachings is evenly divided between those who feel strongly on this matter (15%) and those who are less firm in their view (17%). Just 6% of the adult public says they have no opinion on this matter.

The content of the Bible does not change. Similarly, we have seen no major shift in people's attitudes on the accuracy of Scripture throughout the dozen years we have been assessing this matter. The one pattern that has emerged is a greater polarization of people's views on biblical accuracy. There has been a small up tick? in strong agreement with the notion of biblical accuracy, rising from 35% in 1991 to 42% today. That small increase has come from among the people who previously were lukewarm in their defense if scriptural accuracy. The proportion of adults who give moderate agreement to the concept has declined from 25% in 1991 to 19% now. The combination of strong and moderate support for biblical accuracy has remained unchanged since 1991, though, at about six out of ten adults.

Adult Reactions to the Statement: "The Bible Is Totally Accurate In All That It Teaches"

	1991	1994	1996	1998	2000	2002
Strongly agree	35%	36%	39%	42%	40%	42%
Somewhat agree	25	23	21	19	18	19
Somewhat disagree	11	12	9	8	9	8
Strongly disagree	24	22	25	25	27	24
Don't know	6	7	7	7	7	7

Source: Barna Research Group, Ventura, CA

Who Does – and Does Not – Accept the Bible?

From among the five-dozen subgroups we examined, there are a half-dozen from which 60% or more strongly believe that the Bible's teaching is completely accurate. Those segments include Protestants (61%), blacks (61%), residents of the South (61%), non-evangelical born again adults (66%), political conservatives (63%) and adults who attend churches of 100 or fewer people (60%). We could also add evangelicals to this group, although they are not included in the data table accompanying this section because this question is one of the items used to classify people as an evangelical. In other words, by definition, all evangelicals strongly concur that the Bible is totally accurate in its teachings.

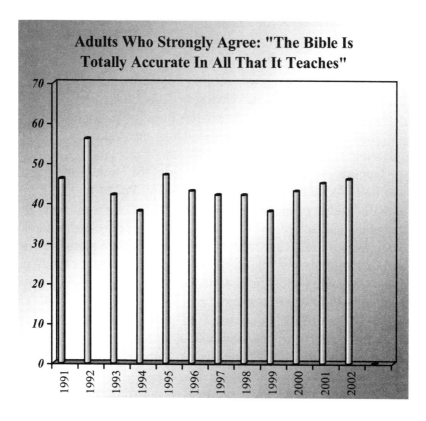

Source: Barna Research Group, Ventura, CA

At the other end of the continuum are the groups that have the lowest proportion of people who strongly affirm the accuracy of Scripture. Segments that have fewer than four out of ten people who accept biblical teaching as reliable include Baby Busters (39%), Catholics (33%), residents of the Northeast (30%), college graduates (31%), people who have never been married (31%Notional Christians (36%), adults of other faith groups (35%), atheists and agnostics (8%),

Independent voters (34%), unchurched adults (25%), political liberals (25%), and Californians (35%).

A Different Spin

In other recent surveys we have asked nationwide samples of adults to describe their views of the Bible in different ways. One tracking approach we use is to ask adults to select one of five statements that comes closest to describing their perception of the Bible. We ask this question every few years but find little change in perceptions over the past decade.

One-quarter of all adults believe that "the Bible is the actual word of God and should be taken literally, word for word." A slightly higher proportion – about one-third – believes that "the Bible is the inspired word of God and has no errors, although some verses are meant to be symbolic rather than literal." One out of six adults say "the Bible is the inspired word of God but there are some factual or historical errors." One out of ten says that "the Bible was not inspired by God but tells us how the writers of the Bible understood God" and the same proportion claims "the Bible is just another book of teachings written by men that contains stories and advice."

One of the most helpful products of our research on Bible perceptions concerns how people from different faith segments react to God's Word. In the table below you will see that there are substantial differences between evangelicals (who believe that the Bible contains no errors), the non-evangelical born agains (three-quarters of whom concur), Notional Christians (only half of whom view the Bible as errorless), and non-Christians (just one-seventh of whom say the Bible can be taken literally or is inspired and errorless).

It is the data regarding the views of non-Christians that provides a real eye-opener with respect to evangelism. With so many outreach strategies relying upon showing non-believers the truths described in the Bible, it is invaluable to realize that a majority of non-Christians reject the authority and truth-basis of scripture from the start.

Some of the demographic patterns related to Bible perceptions are worth noting. The Bible is most likely to be embraced as a text to be taken literally by people living in the South and least likely by those in the West. Adults who attend non-mainline Protestant churches are twice as likely as those associated with mainline or Catholic churches to be inerrantists. Education makes a huge difference, too: adults with a high school education or less are three times as likely as college graduates to take the Bible literally. Blacks are 71% more likely to do so than are whites.

The two positions on the scale that suggest the Bible is always true – that is, the inerrant and infallible positions – are most likely to be adopted by women (24% more likely than men), blacks (37% more likely than whites or Hispanics), churchgoers outside of the Catholic or mainline traditions, people living in the South or Midwest, political conservatives, and Republicans.

"The Bible Is …"

	All	Evan	NEBAC	Not'l	Non-Chr.
actual Word of God, take literally	27%	40%	37%	22%	9%
inspired Word, has no errors, some verses symbolic	31	58	40	27	5
inspired Word, has some factual or historical errors	17	0	14	22	16
not inspired by God, tells how Bible writers understood God	9	0	3	13	14
just another book of teachings by men, stories and advice	10	0	1	10	39

Key: All = all adults   Evan = evangelicals
NEBAC = non-evangelical born again Christians
Not'l = Notional Christians   Non-Chr = non-Christians

Source: Barna Research Group, Ventura, CA

Chapter 15
Earning Salvation

One of the major theological divides in Christendom relates to salvation. Can a person earn eternal salvation? According to our data, it depends whom you ask – and the church affiliation of the individual responding is only loosely associated with their answer.

The Fruits of Goodness

Americans have relatively strong opinions regarding salvation –and, for the most part, they believe that salvation can be earned. A majority of adults have a firm opinion about this issue: 37% strongly agree that salvation can be earned and 29% strongly disagree. When the intensity of belief is overlooked and we combine all adults who concur that salvation can be earned, that segment constitutes the majority (55%).

As the figures in the accompanying table point out, there has been little change on this matter during the past decade. In 1993, 39% strongly agreed that salvation could be earned; today, the figure is 37%, which is statistically equivalent. Ten years ago 26% firmly rejected the notion of earning salvation, compared to a statistically equivalent 29% today. The fluctuations that have occurred in the intervening years have been minor.

Keep in mind that very few people – not quite one in ten – lack an opinion on this matter. From an evangelistic vantage point this suggests that most people who do not rely solely on God's grace provided through the death and resurrection of

Jesus Christ will be hard to reach since they are generally comfortable with their existing doctrine of salvation.

Can A Good Person, Or One Who Does Enough Good for Others, Earn Eternal Salvation?

	1993	1996	1998	2000	2001	2002
Strongly agree	39%	37%	38%	31%	30%	37%
Somewhat agree	17	17	18	20	20	18
Somewhat disagree	8	12	12	11	11	9
Strongly disagree	26	26	26	31	29	29
Don't know	9	8	7	7	9	8

Source: Barna Research Group, Ventura, CA

Demographic Connections

Are you startled to realize that even among non-evangelical born again Christians just four out of ten strongly refute the idea that salvation can be earned? How ironic is it that a majority of those who say that they rely on their own personal commitment to Christ, confession of their sins and individual embrace of Jesus as their savior as the means to salvation concurrently allow for others to receive God's forgiveness and eternal acceptance through their good deeds and best efforts at doing nice things for others? In fact, how credible is the salvation of the one-quarter of the non-evangelical born again adults who have only moderately intense opinions on how salvation works (thus negating the notion of "the assurance" of their salvation) or the other one-fourth-plus who strongly agree that works can earn a place in Heaven?

There are some inexplicable denominational correlations as well. Given the doctrine of the Catholic Church it may be more surprising to find one in five Catholic adults strongly or moderately disagreeing with salvation by works than to find eight out of ten endorsing that approach. It is the Protestant community in which the greatest confusion reigns. In mainline Protestant churches – i.e., Episcopal, Presbyterian Church in the U.S.A. (PCUSA), United Methodist (UMC), Evangelical Lutheran Church in America (ELCA), Lutheran Church – Missouri Synod (LCMS), American Baptist Church (ABC) and United Church of Christ (UCC) – nearly six out of ten adherents (57%) agree that salvation can be earned, while only one-third (34%) reject that idea. Even in the Protestant churches that are not affiliated with the mainline denominations close to half of their adherents (42%) agree that salvation can be earned while barely more than half (53%) dismiss that notion.

The surprises continue in this regard as we examine the statistics among conservatives. This group, while far from synonymous with the elusive (or, perhaps, non-existent) Religious Right, more often than not produces a significant majority of people who embrace biblical standards. Not so in the case of salvation, though. There is an even split among conservatives: 47% take either side of the debate.

Texas, typically the home of adults more inclined to believe the Bible than to bash it, and more likely to attend church than trash it, reflects tremendous confusion in the salvation debate. Six out of ten Texans strongly or moderately agree that salvation can be earned through good works; just 40% resist the notion.

Scrutiny of those who lie at the extremes on this issue – after all, either salvation can be earned or it cannot – no credible systematic theology allows for an either/or choice on this matter – suggests that certain groups are more likely to fall in one camp or the other. The types of adults most commonly numbered among those who strongly argue that salvation is earned include women, non-whites, Catholics and liberals. At the other end of the continuum the anti-works contingent is most likely to be led by Baby Boomers, married adults, non-evangelical born again Christians, Protestant church-goers, and political conservatives.

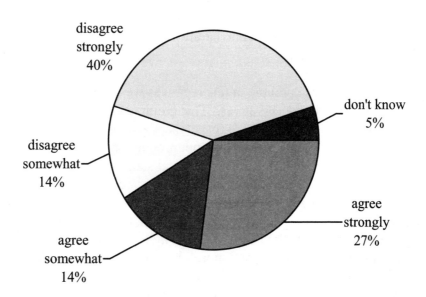

How Non-Evangelical Born Again Christians React to the Notion That A Good Person Will Earn A Place in Heaven

- disagree strongly 40%
- don't know 5%
- disagree somewhat 14%
- agree strongly 27%
- agree somewhat 14%

Source: Barna Research Group, Ventura, CA

Among the surprises highlighted in the table below, however, is the fact that there is not a single demographic subgroup for which a majority strongly dissents from the idea that salvation can be earned. In fact, it is discouraging to note that non-evangelical born again Christians are no less likely than are people of other faiths (e.g. Islam, Judaism, Mormonism) or even atheists and agnostics to strongly argue in favor of salvation by works.

The Extremes: Adults Who Agree or Disagree With Salvation by Works

	Strongly Agree	Strongly Disagree
All adults	37%	29%
Men	31	29
Women	41	29
Baby Busters	38	26
Baby Boomers	35	33
Elders	38	27
Income under $35,000	40	29
Income over $60,000	37	30
Married	35	32
Not married	39	25
White	35	31
Black	41	31
Hispanic	43	22
Non-evangel. born again	27	40
Notional Christian	51	14
Other faith	31	24
Protestant	31	38
Catholic	54	10
Conservative	33	40
Liberal	43	20

Source: Barna Research Group, Ventura, CA

Do not overlook the fact that women are more likely than men to accept salvation by works. Again, this outcome, while consistent over the past decade, is at odds with the typical trend of women adopting more biblically defensible positions than men.

In the end these figures may be a wake up call regarding the clarity and intensity of the teaching that people receive regarding salvation. While evangelicals, by definition, accept the notion of salvation by grace alone, and they are joined by millions of Americans, the undisputable fact is that most Americans consider themselves Christian, believe they will have eternal salvation, and base their view on the notion that salvation can either be a free gift of God or earned through good behavior. Somehow, despite the literally billions of dollars spent on evangelism and Christian education in the past quarter century, the true message of the gospel has failed to penetrate the minds and hearts of most Americans.

Chapter 16
The Responsibility to Evangelize

Millions of Americans take great joy in sharing what they believe could have a positive influence on the lives of other people. For some, that means coaching sports, for others it is critiquing movies, for many it relates to giving money or expertise to help disadvantaged people. And for millions of Americans, it may also include sharing their religious beliefs with people who possess a different perspective on faith matters.

For the better part of the last decade, adults have been evenly divided between those who feel some sense of responsibility to share their religious beliefs with other people (51% in 2002) and those who feel no personal responsibility to tell others what they believe (47%). The actual proportions have see-sawed back and forth during the decade, with one view or the other assuming a tiny edge, but both views consistently hovered within a stones throw of 50% throughout the Nineties and into the early years of the new millennium.

Adults' Views On Having A Personal Responsibility To Tell Other People Their Religious Beliefs

	1996	1998	2000	2002
Agree strongly	31%	29%	31%	35%
Agree somewhat	18	19	17	16
Disagree somewhat	20	21	22	19
Disagree strongly	30	31	28	28

Source: Barna Research Group, Ventura, CA

A subtle change that has overtaken the United States with regard to evangelism in the past two years, though a change that has gone largely unnoticed. What the macro-level statistics have masked is a growing sense of duty among born again Christians to spread their beliefs throughout American society. As shown in the table below, in 1994 only one-third of all non-evangelical born again Christians (36%) strongly affirmed their personal obligation to share their faith. That proportion rose to the low forties throughout the remainder of the Nineties and the initial year of the new decade. Suddenly, for reasons unknown at this time, the percentage of these adults who felt a firm conviction about evangelizing jumped to 49% in 2001 and then to 51% in 2002. About half of the increase can be attributed to non-evangelical born agains who previously felt only a moderate responsibility to evangelize. The other half appears to be due to an evangelistic reawakening among a small but significant portion of the one-third who disagreed as to their duty to share their faith.

How Non-Evangelical Born Again Adults React to the Idea of Having A Personal Responsibility to Tell Their Religious Beliefs to Others

	1994	1996	1998	2000	2001	2002
Agree strongly	36%	43%	42%	42%	49%	51%
Agree somewhat	30	24	25	23	22	20
Disagree somewhat	17	19	21	19	12	16
Disagree strongly	15	13	12	14	14	11

Source: Barna Research Group, Ventura, CA

As noted in chapter 7, there has been no concurrent rise in the actual incidence of evangelistic encounters initiated by all born again adults during the past seven years. What may be happening, then, is that more Christians are undergoing a changed mindset about evangelism now with a pending increase in evangelistic activity to blossom in the days ahead. One can only pray that this is an appropriate interpretation of the conjunction of greater openness to personal engagement in evangelism and the absence of evidence that the change in attitude has produced changed behavior.

Who Accepts the Responsibility?

Not everyone is excited about adopting a more evangelistic posture. Older adults remain the most open to such responsibility, although there has been a noteworthy increase in the number of Busters and Boomers who accept their role in spreading their faith.

The biggest jump in willingness to share their faith, though, has taken place among residents of the South (an increase of 12 percentage points since 1994), Baby Boomers (up 12 points) and Elders (up 11 points). In fact, the growth in evangelistic responsibility would have jumped prolifically if not held back by the very generation that many people cite as being religious: Baby Busters. Since 1994 there has been only a marginal increase among the youngest adults (+3 percentage points). There also appears to have been some growth in openness among Hispanics.

In the end, keep in mind that only half of all non-evangelical born again Christians strongly affirm a personal responsibility to share their faith with others. That is a strong foundation on which to build, but certainly leaves room for growth.

Section 3

Other Measures of America's Faith

Chapter 17: Different Flavors of Christianity
Chapter 18: Teenagers and Their Faith
Chapter 19: Protestant Congregations

Chapter 17
Different Flavors of Christianity

As may be apparent at this point, the term "Christian" means different things to different people. To some, it is synonymous with "American." To others the term refers to a general religious inclination. For many it implies a particular faith orientation, while still others use the term to refer to very specific values, beliefs and lifestyle parameters.

Most Americans are comfortable being called "Christian." For the better part of the past 20 years more than four out of five adults have considered themselves to be Christian, as reflected by the 84% who embraced that label in 2002. That equates to more than 175 million adults – and perhaps another 60 million children – who would attach themselves to the "Christian" moniker. But under that umbrella is a wide range of individuals in terms of the theology, religious practices and lifestyle choices deemed to be consistent with a Christian reality.

Denominational Affiliation

The broadest delineation within the larger Christian community may relate to one's choice of church: Protestant or Catholic. Catholics generally constitute about one-quarter of the adult population; Protestants are usually about three-fifths. In 2002, the statistics showed 21% describing themselves as Catholic and 53% as Protestant. The percentage of individuals who describe themselves as Protestant or who attend a Protestant church has been slowly but steadily dropping for the past two decades. In the early Eighties, some seven out of ten adults were Protestant; the current figure is barely half of the adult mass.

The profile of the Protestant body differs from that of America's Catholics. Based on a combination of seven nationwide studies conducted from January 2000 through January 2002, incorporating interviews with 7044 adults, we discovered several key distinctives.

First, the two groups are quite similar demographically. Catholics are slightly younger, slightly better educated, and include a slightly higher proportion of men. Among the differences, though, are lower divorce rates among Catholics (32% of all Catholics who have ever been married have also been divorced, compared to 41% among Protestants) and a divergent ethnic profile. Twenty-percent of Protestants are black, compared to only 3% of Catholics; 6% of Protestants are Hispanic, whereas four times as many Catholics are of Latino background (28%). Geographic location also differs dramatically. Twenty-nine percent of Catholics live in the Northeast while 16% of Protestants do so. The disparity is compensated for in the South, which contains 42% of all Protestants and just 24% of Catholics. There is also a huge household income gap: the Catholics average income is 18% higher than the average among Protestants. In dollar amounts, Protestant households have a median annual income of $37,508; Catholics have an average of $44,260.

The biggest differences relate to religious behavior and beliefs. As noted in previous chapters of this book, in a typical week Protestant adults are more likely to attend church services, read the Bible, volunteer at church, attend a small group, and attend Sunday school. In a typical year, Protestants are three times more likely to share their faith with someone else. Protestants are also more likely to state that religion is very important in their life; to claim to be absolutely committed to Christianity; to possess an orthodox view of God;

are twice as likely to strongly agree that the Bible is accurate in all of its teachings and to accept personal responsibility for sharing their religious beliefs; and 50% more likely to have made a "personal commitment to Jesus Christ that is still important;" and to strongly disagree that Jesus sinned. Catholics are more likely to strongly agree that Satan is just a symbol of evil and much more likely to affirm that a good person can earn salvation.

The Demographic Profiles of American Protestants and Catholics

	Protestants	Catholics
Median age	44	43
Median household income	$37,508	$44,260
Female	54%	51%
Currently married	55%	56%
Have been married and divorced	41%	32%
Have children under 18 in home	38%	41%
College graduates (4-year degree)	17%	21%
White	71%	67%
Black	20%	3%
Hispanic	6%	28%
Northeast	16%	29%
South	42%	24%
Midwest	24%	25%
West	18%	23%

Source: Barna Research Group, Ventura, CA

It may be of interest to briefly acknowledge the changing shape of denominationalism. In the Protestant realm, Baptists are by far the most numerous: nearly one-third of all adults who attend a Protestant church can be found at some type of

Baptist church. Mainline churches, which once dominated the Protestant scene, have shrunk considerably. Together these churches now attract just 15% of all church-going adults and approximately 30% of the Protestant body. Mainline adherents are allocated roughly as follows: American Baptist at 2%, Episcopal accounting for 3%, Evangelical Lutheran and Lutheran-Missouri Synod a combined 8%, United Methodist attracts 11%, Presbyterian Church U.S.A. is responsible for 4%, and the United Church of Christ gathers 2%.

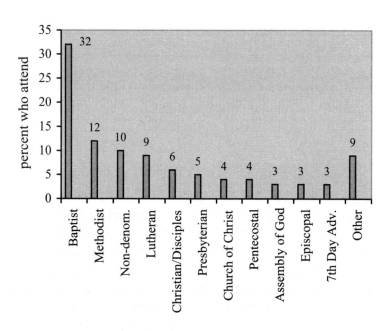

Source: Barna Research Group, Ventura, CA

To give a standard of comparison, the largest non-Baptist, non-mainline Protestant bodies are the non-denominational churches (10%), followed by Christian Churches/Disciples of Christ (6%), Seventh Day Adventist (3%), and Assemblies of God (3%). The remaining one-third of all Protestants is spread among the other 200-plus Protestant denominations in the United States.

Three Segments of Christians

Another way of slicing the portion of the religious pie that encompasses Christians is to categorize people according to the nature of their faith commitment. The smallest of the three Christian segments are the "evangelicals" – a group of individuals who believe that their relationship with Jesus Christ will provide them with eternal life, and who accept a variety of Bible teachings as accurate and authoritative. (For a full description of the definition, refer to the Introduction.)

The second group is "non-evangelical born again Christians," a segment that also believes they have eternal salvation through the grace given them by God through their personal faith in Christ, but who do not believe in various core doctrines taught in the Bible.

The third segment is one that we describe as "Notional Christians." These are people who consider themselves to be Christian, but believe they will have eternal salvation because of some reason other than Christ's death and resurrection for them or, alternatively, claim they do not know their eternal destiny (i.e., whether they will experience eternal life, eternal damnation or some other outcome). These individuals are also less likely than others to embrace core Bible doctrines.

Evangelicals are currently just 5% of the population, non-evangelical born again Christians are 35% and notional Christians are 37%. The rest of the adult population is comprised of individuals who do not think of themselves as

Christian: atheists and agnostics (8% of adults) and adherents of other religious faiths (9%). (The unaccounted for 6% are individuals who do not know how to describe their faith condition and thus remain unclassified.) Because evangelicals are also born again, the total born again Christian population in the U.S. – that is, the combination of evangelicals and non-evangelical born again adults – is presently 40%.

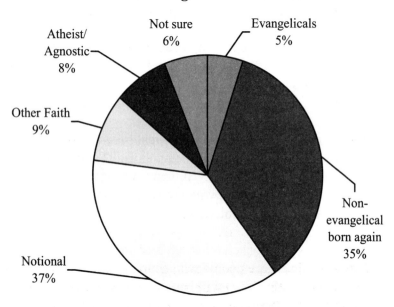

Source: Barna Research Group, Ventura, CA

Evangelicals

The adult evangelical population encompasses some 10 to 12 million adults in the United States. Demographically, they are more likely than most other adults to have a college degree, to be married, to have children under 18 living in their household, and to be white. They are less likely to have experienced a divorce than any of the other faith segments. They were the only segment among the five major faith groups (including people of other faiths and the atheist/agnostic segment) for which a majority is affiliated with the Republican Party. (Keep in mind, however, that "evangelical" is not synonymous with Republican: more than four out of ten evangelicals are <u>not</u> associated with the GOP.) Half of America's evangelicals live in the South and nearly half (45%) are Baby Boomers.

Attitudinally, evangelicals are more than twice as likely as the rest of Americans to describe themselves as "mostly conservative" on social and political issues (71% do so) and they are the least likely segment to describe themselves as "stressed out," "concerned about the future," to be "struggling with debt or finances," or to be actively "searching for meaning and purpose in life."

Evangelicals are vastly different from other adults on moral issues. They are the only group among which a majority (68%) base their moral decisions on the Bible or religious teaching and the sole segment that is more likely to believe in absolute moral truth (58%) than to say that moral choices are relative to the individual and the circumstances (i.e., relativism - 27%). Consequently, their moral views were significantly different from those of every other segment in relation to all 15 of the moral issues examined in the research. They were the least likely to describe cohabitation, gay sex, pornography, profanity, drunkenness, abortion and divorce as morally acceptable behaviors.

As expected, evangelicals are the most active in religious endeavors, ranging from reading the Bible and attending church services to praying, volunteering at their church, attending religious education classes, and participating in a small group for religious purposes. Three out of four shared their faith in Christ with a non-Christian during the past year. Evangelicals are generous donors, too, giving away roughly three times more money during the past year than did the average American adult.

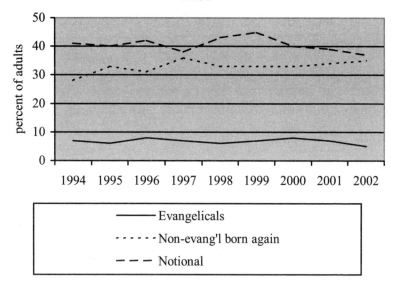

Source: Barna Research Group, Ventura, CA

By definition, evangelicals believe that the Bible is totally accurate in all that it teaches; that they have a responsibility to share their religious faith with others; that their faith is very important in their life; and that God is a real being who is all-knowing, all-powerful and still in control of the world. Nearly nine out of ten believe that the Holy Spirit exists. They also reject several popular theological views: e.g. Jesus sinned during His time on earth, Satan is just a symbol of evil but does not exist, and that being a good person can earn eternal salvation.

Non-Evangelical Born Again Christians

Evangelicals are born again, but most born again Christians are *not* evangelical. (In fact, only one out of five born again adults meet the evangelical criteria.) The 35% of the adult population who are born again but not evangelical represent some 70 to 75 million people. Slightly more than half of them are married, almost three out of four are white, and nearly six out of ten are women. Two out of three live in the South or Midwest.

While many of their attitudes are more similar to those of non-born adults than to those of evangelicals, they do share the evangelical concern about the moral condition of the nation. Only one-third resonates with the label "mostly conservative" and non-evangelical born again adults are slightly more likely to be aligned with the Democratic Party than the Republican Party.

On moral issues, this group is most likely to take its cues from sources other than the Bible or religious teaching. The primary influences on their moral decisions are personal feelings about what is right, the values taught to them by their parents, and whatever choices produce the best personal outcomes. Only one out of every four (27%) contends that moral truth is absolute; more than twice that percentage argue that moral truth is relative to the person and their circumstances. Almost two-thirds consider themselves to be "pro-life," three out of five deem homosexuality to be a morally unacceptable lifestyle, two out of three say movies showing sexually explicit behavior are morally unacceptable, and three-quarters or more say drunkenness, abortion, profanity and gay sex are morally unacceptable behaviors.

Although they are not as active in religious practices as are the evangelicals, a majority of the non-evangelical born again group attends church, reads the Bible, and prays to God during a typical week. Slightly more than half of these adults shared their faith in Christ with a non-Christian during the past year.

The most noticeable difference between evangelicals and the non-evangelical born again segment is in the area of religious beliefs. The largest gaps relate to embracing a responsibility to share their faith in Christ with others, firmly rejecting the idea that Satan is a merely a symbol of evil, describing the Bible as completely accurate in its teachings, rejecting the idea that Jesus Christ sinned while He lived on earth, and strongly denying that the Holy Spirit is just a symbolic representation of God's power or presence (86% of evangelicals do so, compared to only 22% of the non-evangelical born again adults).

Notional Christians

Most adults who describe themselves as "Christian" fall within the boundaries of the "notional" category. While these individuals claim the name Christian, they do not believe that they will have eternal life because of their reliance upon the death and resurrection of Jesus Christ and the grace extended to people through a relationship with Christ. (A large majority of these individuals believe they will have eternal life, but not because of a grace-based relationship with Jesus Christ.) This group represents 37% of all adults in the U.S., which projects to roughly 75 to 80 million adults.

Unlike the two born again segments described above, a majority of the notional Christians are single, and only half are women. These individuals are distributed evenly across the four regions of the nation. Hispanics are especially common in this segment.

One-third of these people say they are stressed out, one-third admits to struggling with debt and finances, and one-third also claims to be searching for a sense of meaning and purpose in life. Just one out of four say they are "mostly conservative" on political and social issues, and Democrats outnumber Republicans by an 8 to 5 ratio. Although four out of five donated money to churches and charities last year, they donated just one-third as much (on a per capita basis) as did evangelicals, and gave barely half as much as the typical non-evangelical born again individual gave away.

Only one out of every ten notional Christians bases moral choices on the Bible or religious teaching, and just one out of every six believes in absolute moral truth. Although half say that abortion should be illegal in all or most circumstances, just 39% consider themselves to be "pro-life." A majority of the people in this segment contends that morally acceptable lifestyles include homosexuality, cohabitation, viewing pornography, and entertaining sexual fantasies.

Even though three-quarters of these people regularly attended a Christian church during their childhood, only a minority regularly attends these days. In a typical week, one out four reads the Bible, one out of three attends a church service, one out of six attends a religious education class, and one out of nine participates in a small group that meets for spiritual purposes.

The religious beliefs of this group stand in stark contrast to those of the two born again segments. For instance, even though they represent about half of all Americans who describe themselves as Christian, just one out of three notional Christians claims to be "absolutely committed" to the Christian faith. One out of three firmly believes that the Bible is totally accurate; just one out of seven (15%) strongly disagrees that Satan is symbolic but not real and a similar proportion (11%) firmly rejects the idea that the Holy Spirit is merely symbolic. A majority contends that eternal life can be earned through good behavior. Only one out of four strongly disagrees with the contention that Jesus committed sins during His tenure on earth.

When Is A Christian Not A Christian?

Scripture is clear that only God knows the hearts of people and that we are therefore not to judge others. The value of research that examines people's faith is not to enable us to pigeonhole or judge them but to give us a better understanding of what people need and how we might best help them to grow in a proper relationship with Christ. Tracking such information throughout the years also provides us with a greater sense of what ministry strategies seem to produce the greatest results.

Recognizing the declining percentage of adults who are evangelicals, and the plateaued percentage of non-evangelical born again adults may motivate you to re-think some of the approaches that you have been using in ministry. It has been said – and proven – that the strategies that got you where you are today will not get you where you need to be tomorrow. Stimulating and empowering people to continue to grow spiritually is a significant albeit difficult challenge. The data emphasize the importance of staying focused on that effort.

Chapter 18
Teenagers and Their Faith

You cannot address the state of the Church without some mention of young people. Children, adolescents and teenagers represent slightly more than two-fifths of the aggregate church community. They are also the emotional and spiritual spark that ignites many congregations and serve as a substantial motivation for millions of adults to return to or stay connected with a church.

Teenagers are a particularly intriguing group to study because they are the hinge that joins the worlds of youth and adults. Between 2001 and 2019 a new generation of Americans will constitute the teenaged population. This new group, whom we have named the Mosaics, is noticeably different than the generation whose members have dominated the teen ranks for the nearly two decades (the Baby Busters).

Teenagers play a crucial role in the development of our nation's core values, economic stability and emphasis, and leadership potential. We have a classic love-hate relationship with teenagers. We love their energy, their creativity, their carefree pursuit of new possibilities, and their indomitable sense of hope. But we dislike their defiance, their ease with change, their unpredictability, and their propensity to challenge what everyone else holds dear.

Regardless of whether we like teenagers or not, they are the future leaders and dominant citizens of the nation – and the emerging leaders and adherents in Christian churches – so it is imperative that while we maximize the available opportunities to influence their values, morals, beliefs and behaviors.

One thing that has not changed much with the passing of the baton from the Busters to the Mosaics is the number of teens who have an interest in faith. For more than a decade, teenagers have been among the most spiritually interested individuals in the nation. However, sensitivity to faith matters has not resulted in a boom in Christian conversions. In fact, while more than three out of five teenagers say they are spiritual, spiritual goals and life outcomes are not among the top-rated goals they have established for their future.

Faith Segments

There is evidence that spirituality has been mainstreamed into teen life without radically affecting the lifestyles and values of most teens. For instance, in 1990 our surveys showed that 31% of teenagers were born again Christians evangelical and non-evangelical combined). In 2001, in spite of increased dialogue about religious matters, a large majority of teens who cite spirituality as a major consideration in life, and the highest levels of church participation by teens during the past quarter century, the teenage born again figure is virtually unchanged at 33%.

Building on the faith categories explored in the preceding chapter, we found that the percentage of teens that are evangelicals has declined from 10% in 1995 to just 4% today. This demise is attributable to growing numbers of teenagers who accept moral relativism and pluralistic theology as part of their faith foundation. The largest percentage of teenagers falls into the notional Christian segment, currently weighing in at 49% of all teens.

Church Affiliation

In recent years there has been very little fluctuation in the denominational affiliations of teenagers. The biggest transition has been a loss of adherents by the Catholic church, dropping from more than 30% adherence among the three Christian segments in the early nineties – and as recently as 1997 and 1998 – to just 22% today. The mainline Protestant churches are standing still after a decade of slow decline, currently drawing about one out of every five teens. Some of those losses have resulted in a small increase in the number of teens associated with charismatic and Pentecostal bodies, although just one out of every ten teens associates with such congregations. (There are tens of thousands more teens, by the way, who are practicing charismatics but attend a non-charismatic church. The charismatic gifts and demonstrations of spiritual power are a perfect fit with a generation that measures value on the basis of personal gain, dramatic experience and entertainment pizzazz.)

The major denominational affiliations of teens have been static in recent years. Since the mid-nineties somewhere in the range of 16% to 18% have been affiliated with Baptist congregations, while other large denominations have showed a similar lack of growth (for instance, the Methodists at 7%, Lutherans at 5%, and Presbyterians at 3%). Barely 2% of the teen population claims to affiliate with a non-denominational church. Although that figure is substantially lower than the proportion among adults, it is more likely that many of the teens are simply unaware of the denominational affiliation of the church they attend and thus claim ignorance of the association.

Christian Commitment

Unexpectedly, given the media hype regarding teen spirituality, our surveys reveal that only three out of every ten self-described Christian teenagers claim to be "absolutely committed" to the Christian faith. The bulk of the teen universe is in the lukewarm category (half say they are "moderately committed"). Even when we focus on the born again teens – the group whose relationship with Christ and understanding of His death and resurrection for their benefit should ignite passionate commitment – we find that just half (48%) claim to be absolutely devoted to the Christian faith.

Typically about six out of ten teenagers say they have made a personal commitment to Christ. Among those individuals about six out of ten believe they will have eternal salvation because of their confession of sins and acceptance of Jesus as their savior. (Thus we arrive at the 33% who are born again, a figure that includes the 4% categorized as evangelical.)

In addition to the aforementioned stagnation in the number of born again teens also notice that among the young people who call themselves Christians and claim to have made a personal commitment to Christ that is important in their life, four out of ten either believe their salvation is based on something other than grace (about 60% of those within this segment) or they do not know what will transpire after their death (the remaining 40%).

What Teenagers Believe

Religious beliefs, regardless of their scriptural veracity, are an integral part of how teens view and cope with life. Four out of five teens say that their religious beliefs are very important in their life. But what do they believe?

As is true among adults, most teenagers (96%) say that they believe in God. That raises the tougher question of "what god?" Two-thirds of them believe in the God described in the Bible – the all-powerful, all-knowing, perfect creator of the universe who rules the world today. The remaining one-third is split between a variety of new age, narcissistic and eastern views of divinity. Eight percent believe that God refers to the total realization of personal, human potential, while a similar number contend that God represents a state of higher consciousness that a person may reach. Five percent believe in multiple gods, each of whom possesses different power and authority. Only a handful (4%) believes that every individual is god, and just 4% state that there is no such thing or being as God. The remaining teens still have not come to a conclusion about the existence or nature of God.

Four out of every five teens contend that God created the universe and just as many say that God is personally involved in people's lives. In a demonstration of the power of the pluralist argument, two-thirds also believe that Muslims, Buddhists, Christians, Jews and all other people pray to the same god, even though they may use different names for their deity of choice.

Few teens doubt the existence of Jesus Christ or His virgin birth, but most of them believe that when He was on earth Jesus committed sins. (Sadly, there is shockingly little difference between the views of born again and non-born again teens on this matter.)

Although teenagers are attracted to the supernatural they are also dubious as to the existence of the Holy Spirit and Satan. Two-thirds of all teenagers (68%) deny the existence of the Holy Spirit, saying that it is merely a symbol of God's presence or power but is not a living entity. Similarly, two out of every three teens (65%) contend that Satan is not a living being but is a symbol of evil. On both of these important theological issues, the views of born again teens are indistinguishable from those of their non-born again peers.

Given the beliefs already outlined it should not be surprising to learn that teenagers are confused about what to believe regarding the Bible. On the one hand, six out of ten say that the Bible is totally accurate in all of its teachings. They tend to believe that it is a valuable tool for moral discernment and guidance and embrace the validity of many of the fundamental teachings contained in the Bible. However, three-quarters of them state that a central message of the Bible is that God helps those who help themselves. Few of them rely upon the Bible for moral truth in their personal lives, and the uniqueness of the Bible is overlooked, too: close to six out of ten teens posit that all religious faiths teach equally valid truths.

Things do not become any clearer when the subject is salvation: contradictions abound regarding humankind's nature and spiritual needs. Three-fourths of all teenagers believe that God judges everyone after death, six out of ten say that forgiveness of sins is possible only through faith in Jesus Christ, and just one in five believes that there are some sins that we commit that not even God can forgive. At the same time, however, only one out of every three teens accept the biblical teaching that people who do not consciously accept Jesus Christ as their savior will be condemned to hell. Three out of every five believe that if a person is generally good, or does enough good things for others during their life, they will earn a place in Heaven. Even half of all born again teenagers believe that a person can earn their way into Heaven.

Faith is significant to teenagers, though, in the sense that eight out of every ten believe that their religious faith is very important in their life and almost as many (seven out of ten) claim that the Christian faith is relevant to their life today. Nearly three-quarters of American teens are able to recall specific times recently when their religious beliefs actually changed the way they normally would have behaved.

Yet, half of all teens believe it does not matter what religious faith you associate with because all of the major faith groups believe the same principles and truths. We may also have reason to wonder if teens are truly open to spiritual growth and life change since two-thirds claim that they are already very familiar with all of the major principles and teachings of the Christian faith and three-fourths contend that they are not likely to change what they believe in the future.

Religious Behavior

To the shock of many adults we have found that teens have higher levels of participation in organized religious activity than do adults! This is not due to parental mandate as much as it is borne out of a desire to share significant experiences with a cherished peer group – that is, with the closest friends, or tribe, of the individual. There seems to be a fairly simple but powerful principle that has fueled such widespread church involvement among teens: where the leaders of the group go, so go its individual members.

Religious Activity in the Past 7 Days
(base: self-described Christians or those who attend a Christian church)

activity	1990	1997	1998	1999	2000	2001
attend a church service	54%	52%	53%	56%	52%	53%
read from the Bible	33	34	33	35	36	39
a church-based youth group activity or event	29	37	35	32	36	37
Sunday school class	NA	35	39	35	40	35
faith-based small group	NA	30	27	29	28	33
pray to God	NA	81	80	89	84	83

Source: Barna Research Group, Ventura, CA

The degree of teenaged religious activity is laudable. Among teens who describe themselves as Christian or who attend a Christian church, half attend a worship service during a typical weekend; one-third read from the Bible during a typical week, excluding when they are at a church service or event; four out of five pray to God during an average week; approximately one out of three attends youth group activities at the church during a typical week; and roughly the same percentages are involved in a Sunday school class in a typical weekend and show up for a small group that meets sometime during the week. There have been minor fluctuations in these statistics throughout the course of the decade, but overall there has been no net change in these indicators for about a decade.

Although young people go to great lengths to declare and to demonstrate their independence and control of their lives, the data show a remarkable resemblance between adults and teenagers in terms of weekly religious activity. There is no significant difference between the two groups in relation to prayer and Bible reading, and the gaps related to worship service attendance, Sunday school involvement and small group participation are minor. In each case, teenagers are higher on the activity scale than are adults.

A Comparison of the Religious Activity of Adults and Teenagers, in a Typical Week

activity	teens	adults
prayed to God	83%	81%
attended a church service	53	43
read from the Bible	39	42
attended a Sunday school class	35	25
participated in a small group	33	18

Source: Barna Research Group, Ventura, CA

Involvement in a Church Youth Group

About two-thirds of all teenagers have some interaction with a church youth program during the course of a typical month. Translated into aggregate numbers that means of the 22 million teens in the U.S. nearly 15 million have some exposure to Christianity through youth groups in an average month. A significant, if minority, portion of that number is comprised of individuals who do not consider themselves to be Christian, and another significant share is made up of notional Christians. This latter group constitutes half of the kids who experience a church's youth group in a given month – a pool of more than 7 million unsaved kids who embrace the Christian name but not its core truths.

Keep in mind that this prolific church attendance does not suggest an intense desire to worship and learn about God so much as it reflects a commitment to their friends. When we asked teens why they get involved in church activities, the overwhelming motivation was being with their friends. Half of them listed the presence of their friends, making personal relationships three times the attraction of any other factor listed. Other important elements included the opportunity to learn about God and the Christian faith (mentioned by one out of four) and the activities and events that take place (listed by one out of five). Reasons such as the charisma of the youth leader, the music or the opportunity to experience God's presence were rarely identified as their motivations.

Teenagers are savvy consumers, though, and also indicated that they would not hang out with their friends at a church unless they have some reason to believe that the church will produce some value for them. In other words, relationships are the primary focus but spiritual substance and developing community are critical deliverables. Gaining practical knowledge about God was listed twice as often as anything else as the most important reason for returning. The fellowship, the games, the music, the casual and friendly atmosphere may attract kids once or twice, but instigating regular participation requires some level of solid, personally applicable content.

Future Church Attendance

Even though teens are active in church life and spiritual pursuits today, they do not expect to remain that active once their lives become more independent and career-driven.

When asked to predict some of their lifestyle changes once they graduate from high school or move away from home, surprisingly few contend that they will attend a Christian church on a regular basis. Based on some statistical modeling techniques we have developed to estimate likely behavior it seems likely that about one out of three teenagers will attend a Christian church after they leave home. If this estimate is even close to accurate, it signals future struggles for the Church. A drop of 50% in the attendance of any generation would have a devastating impact on the American Church.

No matter what the rate of attendance winds up being among Mosaics as they reach adulthood, they are likely to change the face of the church world. You may be aware that they have little loyalty to institutions – remember, they are more likely to attend church because of relationships than for spiritual sustenance – and tend to "church hop" frequently. They do not necessarily limit themselves to a particular type of religious experience – e.g., Protestant, Catholic, Christian, church-based, worship service – but enjoy the variety of religious expressions that their diverse theological perspectives allow.

The type of church that might be most attractive to them in the future depends upon their spiritual inclinations. Teens who consider themselves to be Christian were most interested in the church's internal culture, the depth of community among congregants and the quality of the spiritual substance provided by the church. In contrast, among teens that do not think of themselves as Christian the most appealing facets are the presence of their friends in the church, convenient location, the level of trust and care evident among congregants, and service to the poor of the community.

Thankfully, one of the core factors they seek is having an authentic experience with God and other people. Teenagers patronize churches and other event-oriented organizations because they are seeking a compelling experience that is made complete and safe by the presence of people they know and trust, and from whom they are willing to learn and take their cues.

Teens Are Misunderstood Spiritually

The presence of teenagers on church campuses and their frequent discussions regarding spirituality are generally misinterpreted by adults to mean that teens are deeply and indefatigably spiritual. In reality, teens demand transcendent adventures and supportive relationships. Community is a core dimension of the Christian faith and one that the Mosaic and Buster generations prioritize. They seek outlets for impacting the lives of other people and influencing the direction of their corner of reality, balancing compassion and selfishness in a new blend of social awareness.

Churches that provide a conduit for serving others while facilitating true community and genuine experiences with God will attract and bond with the Mosaic generation. Because Mosaics will make the rules that define their religious choices connecting with them will not be easy. Then, again, it has never been easy for the Church to understand, embrace and nurture an emerging generation.

Chapter 19
Protestant Congregations

There are an estimated 320,000 Protestant churches in America today, a number that rises and falls daily with the shutting down of anemic congregations and the launching on new churches. In spite of this continual burying and birthing process, the aggregate profile of Protestant churches in the U.S. remains quite stable from year to year.

Church Attendance

The average number of adults attending services at a Protestant church during a typical week in 2001 was 90, the same total as measured in 2000. This reflects a 10% decline from the 1997 level of 100 adults and a 12% drop from the attendance average in 1992.

Church attendance was highest in the South, where the typical church has 100 adults who show up, while the lowest figures were recorded in the Northeast and West, each region averaging 80 adults. The Midwest fell in the middle, with 90 adults participating in a typical week.

Churches associated with charismatic denominations (such as Assembly of God, United Pentecostal or Foursquare) had the lowest average turnout (80), while black congregations had the highest median attendance (120). Mainline churches were above the norm (98), as were churches described as "seeker-driven" (100). Baptist churches, which comprise the most prolific category of churches in America, were consistent with the national average (90).

An intriguing anomaly is that churches affiliated with a charismatic denomination attract an average of just 80 adults, but churches described as charismatic by their pastor but that are not aligned with a charismatic denomination attract more adults than either the national average for Protestant churches or the norm for charismatic churches. Those churches – a combination of mainline, independent and evangelical congregations – average 150 adults per week, which is nearly 90% more than denominational charismatic churches.

Church Finances

The typical operating budget of Protestant churches for the past year was about $115,000. That is nearly $5,000 higher than in 2000, and represents a rise that slightly exceeds the increase attributable to cost-of-living jump. The figures exclude funds donated to special funds, such as building campaigns.

The churches that have the largest operating budgets were those in the South (median: $130,000), while the smallest budgets were found among churches in the Midwest ($96,000). On a per capita basis, churches in the West received the highest amount of funding, while churches in the Midwest garnered the smallest per capita giving.

Theological Leanings

Most Protestant pastors describe their church as "evangelical" (83%) and as "theologically conservative" (79%). While a majority says theirs is "seeker-sensitive" (54%), only one-third say their church is "seeker-driven" (34%). Four out of ten claim their congregation is "fundamentalist" (40%), while lesser proportions claim the descriptions "charismatic" (23%), "Pentecostal" (22%), or "theologically liberal" (13%).

Mainline churches – with the exception of United Methodist and American Baptist churches – comprise the bulk of the congregations that adopt the label "theologically liberal." (Most United Methodist and American Baptist embrace the term "evangelical" and are much more likely to say they are theologically conservative than theologically liberal.)

Among the churches that claim to be "seeker-driven" nearly half are located in the South and about half describe themselves as "fundamentalist."

Pastoral Compensation

The median value of pastoral compensation for America's Senior Pastors is presently $38,214. (Pastoral compensation is a mixture of salary and benefits, such as housing allowance, car allowance, insurance, and retirement payments. Current laws make it advantageous for pastors to receive part of their compensation as housing and auto allowances, thereby reducing their taxable income.) That is a 19% increase since 1992 – significant in dollars, but still lagging inflation during that period. In other words, despite the rise in compensation, pastors effectively earn less today, based on constant dollars, than they earned a decade ago.

The low levels of clergy compensation are especially noteworthy because more than two-thirds of all Senior Pastors have a graduate-level degree. Other professionals with that level of education earn average salaries of $60,000 or more, depending upon their profession. However, many church-goers *expect* their pastor to earn less than the national average because they are involved in ministry, regardless of their school loans and family obligations. Pastors who have a seminary degree receive an average compensation package of $42,083 – significantly above the average for pastors without a seminary degree ($31,500), but notably below the national norm for professionals with advanced degrees.

The highest-paid pastors are those serving the largest congregations: for instance, the median income among pastors whose church has more than 250 adult attenders is $56,429 annually. (Recognize that these churches represent less than one-fifth of the Protestant congregations in the country.) Pastors of churches with less than 100 adults earn, on average, just $29,808 annually.

Other pastors whose income is above average for the profession include those leading mainline congregations ($41,364), seminary graduates ($42,083), pastors with more than 10 years of experience in full-time ministry ($42,035), and those leading a congregation in the West ($40,313).

Among the lowest-paid pastors are those serving churches in charismatic denominations ($36,591) as well as those pastoring black congregations ($36,875). Other low-paid segments included pastors who have been in full-time ministry less than five years ($35,667), Baby Busters (i.e., pastors under 37 years of age – averaging $33,438), and pastors who have not graduated from seminary ($31,500).

The research also points out that Senior Pastors in suburban ($42,500) and urban ($42,424) churches earned more than their counterparts who lead rural congregations ($33,456). This is largely a consequence of the small size of most rural congregations.

Senior pastors with seminary degrees represent two-thirds of the pastors in the Northeast (67%) but just half of those in the West (49%). Such degrees are most common among mainline pastors (89%) but unusual among pastors of churches associated with charismatic denominations (29%) or black churches (48%).

Pastoral Background

The demographic profile of Protestant pastors has changed little during the past decade. Most pastors are male (95%), married (94%), have graduated from seminary (60%). Relatively few (13%) have ever been divorced – half the rate among their parishioners. The median age of pastors is 49. On average, they have been in full-time ministry for 17 years, and have been pastoring their current church for 5 years.

While some churches have bi-vocational pastors (i.e. they receive their income from an outside job, pastoring the church without pay or for partial pay) or part-time pastors, 87% of Protestant churches have full-time, paid pastors. However, only one out of every four churches has more than one pastor on the payroll. Often, when a church has multiple pastors, a youth pastor is among those paid for ministry. Even so, just one out of every five Protestant churches (19%) has a full-time, paid youth pastor. This reflects the limited number of teenagers who attend the average church: 15. Full-time, paid youth pastors are least common in the Northeast and in black congregations. Less than one out of every twenty Protestant churches has a youth ministry that attracts 100 or more teenagers.

Most Senior Pastors say they have the spiritual gift of preaching or teaching (63%). No other gift is mentioned by half as many pastors. Other gifts named by significant numbers of pastors included pastoring (28%), administration (13%), prophecy (13%), leadership (11%), evangelism (8%). Leadership was most likely to be identified by pastors serving in the West (18%), by those in Baptist churches (15%), and by pastors under age 35 (22%). The leadership gift was least likely to be claimed by pastors in the South (9%), those in mainline congregations (9%), and by pastors over the age of 50 (9%).

Interestingly, Baby Boomers (the group born between 1946 and 1964) now dominate the pastorate. Among all adults in the country, Boomers represent nearly four out of every ten adults. However, Boomers now hold 61% of all Senior Pastor positions in the nation. Their predecessors, the Baby Busters (born 1965 to 1983), constitute about one-third of the adult population, but currently fill just 7% of the pastorates in America.

One of the most interesting comparisons is between male and female pastors. While women represent just 5% of all Protestant Senior Pastors, there is great dissimilarity in the backgrounds of these two groups. Female pastors are much more likely to be seminary-trained (86% have a seminary degree, compared to 60% of male pastors); are more than twice as likely to have been divorced (31%, compared to 12% among male pastors); have less experience in the pastorate (9 years in full-time paid ministry, compared to a median of 17 years among men); last less time in a given church than do men (three years per pastorate, compared to almost six years among men); are almost four times more likely to describe themselves as theologically liberal (39% vs. 11%, respectively); much less likely to embrace the label of "evangelical" (58%, vs. 85% among male pastors); and receive much lower compensation packages.

The Big Picture

To fully appreciate pastors' contribution keep in mind that church-goers expect their pastor to juggle an average of 16 major tasks. That's a recipe for failure – nobody can handle such a wide range of responsibilities while remaining sane and effective. Ultimately, the only way a pastor can succeed in church-based ministry is to create a team of gifted and compatible believers who work together to love people and to pursue a commonly held vision from God. Pastors who strive to meet everyone's demands and keep everyone happy inevitably fail in one way or another.

The trend line of church tenure continues to show that many pastors are not given an adequate opportunity to shine. Relying on a variety of key measures we have learned that the typical pastor has his or her greatest ministry impact at a church in years five through fourteen of their pastorate. Unfortunately, the average pastor lasts only five years at a church, thereby forfeiting the fruit of their investment in the church they've pastored. In our fast turnaround society where we demand overnight results and consider everyone expendable and everything disposable, we may be shortchanging pastors – and the congregations they oversee – by prematurely terminating their tenure.

Pastoring is far from being the easy, low-pressure job that many congregants assume it to be. The typical Protestant Senior Pastor works 55 to 60 hours per week, often working under high pressure and with limited resources at his disposal. Pastors are constantly on-call, often sacrifice time with family to tend to congregational crises, carry long-term debt from the cost of seminary, and generally receive below-average compensation in return for performing a difficult job. Trained in theology, they are expected to master leadership, politics, finance, management, psychology and conflict resolution. Sometimes it seems miraculous that we have anyone left in the pastorate!

Section 4

Charting the Course

Chapter 20
Challenges to the Church

Every organization or institution that strives to influence the way that people think and behave must be nimble. In an age where change is so continual and systemic that it becomes invisible, the entities that prevail are those that intentionally focus on understanding and addressing current and coming conditions. Constant adjustments are mandated if longevity and impact are desired attributes of the movement.

The portrait of America's faith depicted in the preceding pages is simultaneously depressing, encouraging, scary and exciting. The appropriate response must be to rely upon God for guidance and then to do the work of the Church – exploiting opportunities for His purposes and overcoming barriers to spiritual growth that arise. By way of summary, allow me to identify nine core issues that this book has pointed out as challenges facing the Christian Church in America in these early years of the new millennium.

Challenge #1: The Same Old Same Old

Did it strike you as odd that there has not been a more dramatic series of changes in people's religious behavior and beliefs during the past decade? Little else in our lives has remained static during that period. People buy different products, entire industries have come and gone, relational networks have been revolutionized by entertainment and communications innovations, political ideology has been on a roller-coaster ride, globalization and personalization have changed our worldviews, and leadership has morphed from autocratic to team-based forms. How is it, then, that the look and experience of the Christian Church remained so unaffected?

Sadly, the answer may be that Americans treat the faith dimension as one area in which predictability and stability are desirable. That is fine – except that it robs the faith dimension of dynamism. Religious energy may be experienced through new forms of music or dramatic architecture, but there is a noteworthy staleness to the faith experience of most Americans. Bluntly stated, we typically maintain a loose trust in a generic god for unspecified purposes, demonstrated by going through the motions at faith centers on a semi-regular basis.

Nothing could have substantiated this view more clearly than America's response to the terrorist crisis of September 11, 2001. During the first several weeks after the attacks on New York and the nation's capitol there was a surge in church attendance and prayer. Within a matter of weeks, though, that sense of urgency had died and people returned to their typical life patterns. Post-attack surveys showed that people had turned to churches as a place to be with others and to gain a sense of community, solidarity and stability. Shockingly, God had little to do with the comfort and security derived.

If Christianity is to be a serious component in people's lives there must be an intentional and strategic shake-up of what we do and how we do it within our faith communities. More of the same won't get us any farther down the road of genuine discipleship.

Challenge #2: The Decline of the Evangelicals

Thanks to media reports that have distorted and harshly criticized them, evangelicals are a group that many Americans have grown to distrust and dislike. However, for Americans to adopt such feelings toward the group is to miss the point.

Whether you like them or not, the reality is that the declining numbers of evangelicals reflect a deterioration of Bible-based faith in America. Say what you will about evangelicals and their goals, their demise signals the rise of postmodernism within the Church itself.

In our studies, we do not categorize people as "evangelicals" because they claim that label; people are defined as such on the basis of their theological beliefs. The diminution of the group suggests that aberrant theology and doctrine are increasingly invading the inner circle of the Bible-believing community, much less the ranks of faith groups that base their beliefs on influences other than Scripture.

Whether you applaud evangelicals or abhor them, recognize the implications of their marginalization. Every day, the Church is becoming more like the world it allegedly seeks to change. At what point does that collapse become a "crisis" and merit concentrated and strategic response?

Challenge #3: Ethnic Ascension

A careful reading of this book shows just how different the major ethnic groups in America relate to God and faith. The recent Census of the American population confirmed that the bulk of the growth in our nation is attributable to immigration and to the higher birth rates within ethnic families. Sociologists agree that the expansion of ethnic populations in the U.S. will continue for several decades to come, even suggesting that half of the population will be non-white by the time we reach the mid-point of this century.

How will the Church address the extreme ethnic diversification of faith communities? Most efforts at building multi-ethnic or multi-cultural churches have failed for various reasons. Planting new churches designed to reach a particular non-white ethnic group may not do much toward building a true Church. Of the five generations living side-by-side in America today, the Mosaics seem most comfortable with multi-cultural institutions and endeavors. How can we translate that openness into a church that is truly color blind and authentically biblical?

Challenge #4: What About the Bible?

In the last quarter century it seems that we have learned how to sell Bibles but not how to sell what's in the Bible. Increasingly, people pick and choose the Bible content they like or feel comfortable with, but ignore the rest of God's counsel. This tendency seems especially prolific among young adults and teenagers.

The Church without the Bible as its foundation is like building a chair without legs – it lacks the key physical element required to provide strength and value. Amidst the politically popular calls for diversity, tolerance and pluralism, what can we do to elevate the prominence, credibility and perceived value of God's Word in the eyes of a fickle and distracted public?

Challenge #5: A Costless Faith

Americans know all about Jesus but surprisingly few know Him. Can you imagine really knowing Him and being merely lukewarm about being His disciple? That's exactly what we have in the U.S., though, as evidenced by the preponderance of notional Christians – and even the lackadaisical spirituality of millions of non-evangelical born again Christians.

My interpretation of this condition is that we have simply made it too easy to be part of the Church. Christianity has no cost in America. In fact, we've made it way too easy to be "born again" – perhaps much easier than Jesus intended.

Consider this: in the 1960s, Boomers were angry about the hypocrisy of religious institutions and individuals, and shunned the church world. Today, nearly half of the born again adults and a majority of Protestant pastors are Boomers. What happened? It has less to do with Boomers having children and wanting their offspring to have religion than it has to do with savvy consumerism. Boomers, after all, are the wealthiest, best-educated and the most consumption-oriented generation in the nation's history. So when it came to the faith arena, what happened? They played *Let's Make A Deal*.

Boomers were exposed to faith-based marketing pitches that offered them eternal salvation as a free gift if they would simply say the required prayer. "God loves you, humankind blew the relationship, but He has a plan for your life; just saying the magic words triggers the contract" was the essential message of the offer. Boomers studied the offer and realized it was a no-lose proposition: eternal security at nothing down, no future payments, just simple verbal assent. The deal specified nothing about life change – sure, there were some vague promises about this being the best decision one could ever make and how it would change a person's life forever, but there were no detailed requirements or sacrifices demanded.

The result has been a transaction consummated with tens of millions of Americans in which the "free gift" of salvation was claimed with no substantive reciprocation – no commitment, no change, no responsibility. In essence, we lost sight of the fact that to truly embrace this precious gift of God's Son, we must be like Him in personal *brokenness*. But our research shows that few "born again" Christians, despite having some appropriate doctrinal notions and having said the requisite prayer, never experienced the deep spiritual brokenness that enabled them to realize Jesus Christ was, is and will forever be their only hope of experiencing genuine meaning, purpose and salvation. Instead of broken people eternally grateful for the sacrifice and grace extended to them, we have millions of people who have simply tried to exploit God – people for whom salvation is little more than a fire insurance policy they won't think about until the Devil comes knockin'. In the interim we witness a "born again" population that is indistinguishable from the rest of the nation – and has very limited credibility when it comes to promoting genuine Christianity.

The American Church is the world's primary exporter of cheap grace. At some point, though, poor products come back to haunt the producer. Welcome to the haunting time.

At what stage do we bite the bullet and acknowledge that God does not need a majority to accomplish His will, instead He seeks people who will surrender their own grand plans in order to live for Him? When do we get to the point at which we accept smaller numbers of intensely devoted people rather than feverishly investing in filling auditoriums and stadiums with massive numbers of the lukewarm "Christians" that Jesus promised to spew from His mouth (Rev. 3:16)? What might cause us to acknowledge that, yes, faith in God is good, but even the demons believe in God – and that it takes more than a naïve, inch-deep faith in Christ to become part of a Church that truly honors God?

Challenge #6: Understanding the Supernatural

To millions of Americans, "supernatural" refers to the name of a popular recording by Carlos Santana. To millions more the idea of supernatural powers brings to mind the "harmless" adventures of Harry Potter or the imaginative exploits in *Lord of the Rings*. Shockingly few Americans understand the power and significance of the supernatural world – the real supernatural dimension.

You cannot win a war if you deny the existence of your enemy. Similarly, you cannot win a battle if you refuse to use your primary weapons. Yet, that is the state of the Christian Church today. Most Americans deny the existence of Satan and the Holy Spirit and are blissfully ignorant of the spiritual battle the rages around and within them. People dabble with the fringes supernatural experience but dismiss the realities of the supernatural world and its personal implications.

If the Christian Church is to be the positive power source that Jesus intended, and to wage the good fight against evil, we cannot enter the battle unarmed and ignorant. Who will inform and motivate God's people about the realities of the battle?

Challenge #7: New Form and Substance

Say what you will about teenagers, but they do exert substantial influence on our culture. You can see their fingerprints all over the entertainment industry, the Internet, public schools, the fashion world and the family. If you look closely, you will also see their escalating impact on the style and substance of the Church, too.

Mosaics are the first of the postmodern generations. Busters introduced the ideas and lifestyles of that worldview, but Mosaics are immersed in postmodernism. Aided by the rise of Busters in the pastorate, Mosaics will question and then reshape much of the theology that many churches embrace. And they will alter the very ways in which the community of saints gather and experience God's and each others' presence.

You can count on some foundation-rattling challenges coming from the Mosaics. Are you ready?

Challenge #8: Isolation Amidst Plenty

In chapter 19 you read that there are more than 300,000 Protestant churches in the U.S. There are another 20,000 Catholic churches that can be added to the mix. Certainly the

U.S. has no lack of religious way stations. We have many times more outposts than serve the mission of the Postal Service (there are less than 50,000 post offices), the public schools (we have roughly 91,000 elementary and secondary schools) or McDonald's (less than 15,000 locations). Yet, the Church has less impact on our culture than any of those less prolific entities, despite missions that are much less significant or compelling. We do not lack churches; we lack churches that are maximizing their potential to positively influence lives for Christ.

Why aren't churches more influential? There are many reasons, of course, but one that must be addressed is the isolation of each church from the other religious outposts. Too often, the Christian churches in America operate like independent contractors or individual fiefdoms rather than determined members of a grand movement, united by a common cause and leader. In many communities churches compete rather than cooperate. In some circles believers exhibit disdain rather than love for those who represent different Christian traditions.

God has not called churches into existence so that they can build their own kingdoms; each has been assigned a role within His kingdom. For us to expect a typical outpost of 90 adults working with a $115,000 budget to single-handedly initiate and facilitate a moral and spiritual revolution, even within just its community, is ludicrous.

What will it take for churches to become The Church? At what point will we drop our territorialism and recognize how much we need each other in order to complete God's work His way?

Challenge #9: Where Are the Leaders?

Churches all over the country are crying out for strong, visionary, godly leadership. The people who fill the positions of leadership in churches today are, for the most part, teachers – good people, lovers of God, well-educated, gifted communicators – but not leaders. They do not have or understand vision. They are incapable of motivating and mobilizing people around God's vision. They fail to direct people's energies and resources effectively and efficiently. The Church suffers for this absence of genuine leadership.

Pastors themselves are not to blame. They have emerged from a system that so esteems scholarly pursuits that leadership has been left by the wayside, and the Church has suffered accordingly. In the future, for the Church to become strong again we must heed the guidance of the leaders God has called and gifted for that purpose, while growing through the focused teaching of those who are gifted to explicate His Word and its profound implications for our lives. The failure to do so will result in greater unnecessary setbacks and suffering for the Church in this nation.

No Easy Road

There is no easy road for us to pursue en route to restoring the Church to health. It has taken us many years and millions of hours of work to bring the Church to its current position and it will undoubtedly take millions of hours of prayer and hard work to return to a place of greater spiritual health. The resuscitation of the Christian Church in America is not an overnight proposition: it is a multi-generational, multi-decade task that must begin today if we hope to have grandchildren and great grandchildren who will mature in a healthier spiritual environment than we have at the present time.

Accurate awareness of our condition and the emerging opportunities is certainly a key factor in turning the Church around. It is my fervent prayer that this book provides some of the information you need to take appropriate steps to honor God and His people through your ministry.

Appendix

Research Methodology
Related Resources
About the Author
About the Barna Research Group, Ltd.

Research Methodology

This book is based on data derived from nationwide surveys among adults conducted by the Barna Research Group, Ltd. of Ventura, California every January. In each survey a random sample of adults was drawn from the 48 continental states and a survey questionnaire was administered to qualified individuals. These telephone surveys, known as OmniPoll™ were conducted from the Barna Research field facility in southern California. The surveys among teenagers, also conducted through the use of a random sampling of households that were screened to locate people 13 to 18 years of age, were conducted from the Barna Research interviewing facility and were based on interviews with 600 to 615 teenagers in each year's survey. The surveys among Protestant Senior Pastors involved random samples of 602 to 610 pastors. The timing and related statistics pertaining to those surveys are shown below:

Year	Adult surveys sample size	Teen surveys sample size	Pastor surveys sample size
2002	1006	N/A	N/A
2001	1005	604	601
2000	1002	605	601
1999	1002	614	604
1998	1006	605	610
1997	1007	--	601
1996	1004	--	--
1995	1005	723	--
1994	1204	--	--
1993	1203	--	--
1992	1009	--	--
1991	1003	--	--
1990	N/A	405	--

All of the surveys among adults and teenagers that were incorporated into the analysis were conducted through the use of random digit dial sampling technique. In this method we derive a representative nationwide sample of telephone numbers that have been randomly generated. We then call the household and screen respondents to determine whether or not a qualified person lives in the home. If so, we attempt to conduct the interview with them. While we are not able to connect with every eligible adult whose home we call, our response rates in qualified households exceed industry norms. In these surveys, the response rates ranged from 61% to 76% in qualified households. The average survey lasted anywhere from 15 to 22 minutes per respondent.

The maximum amount of sampling error associated with each adult survey is plus or minus three percentage points at the 95% confidence level. The maximum sampling error associated with the different subgroups alluded to in the text varies with their sample size. The maximum sampling error for the surveys among teenagers and Senior Pastors is plus or minus four percentage points at the 95% confidence level.

Related Resources

As you read this book, other questions may have been raised. Often, Barna Research has produced related resources that may answer those questions that you have. Here are a few related resources to consider:

A Fish Out of Water
A practical guide to handling the common problems leaders face, ranging from identifying whether or not you are a leader, to handling vision, conflict, team-building, organizational lifecycles, character issues, and more.

Power of Team Leadership
An examination of the value of teams, the types of leaders that produce great teams, and the process of transitioning a church from individual-based to team-based leadership.

Christian Leader Profile™
Have you ever wondered if you are a leader, and if you are, how you measure up? The Profile will help you discern if and how God has called you to lead.

Boiling Point
A look ahead to the year 2010, describing the cultural shifts occurring and their implications for Christian ministry.

The Habits of Highly Effective Churches
Based on a multi-year research project, this book details the ministry practices that characterize the most effective ministries in the nation.

Growing True Disciples
Based on studies among born again Christians and among Senior Pastors, this book describes what Christians believe and how churches are effectively discipling believers.

Real Teens
The first comprehensive examination of the Mosaic generation, looking at the attitudes, lifestyles, goals, religious practices and beliefs of teenagers.

The Barna Update
This is a bi-weekly e-mailed notification of the latest report by George Barna. The e-mail identifies the topic and primary areas of focus in each newly-released report. Those reports can then be read or downloaded directly from the Barna Research website. There is no cost for this service. Sign up on the home page of the website (www.barna.org).

These and many other resources are available to assist you in ministry. For more information about any of these resources, or others that may be useful, please go to the Barna Research Group website at www.barna.org. Orders may also be placed through 1-800-55-BARNA during business hours Monday through Friday, Pacific time.

About the Author
George Barna

George Barna is the founder and Directing Leader of the Barna Research Group, Ltd., a marketing research firm located in Ventura, CA. The company specializes in conducting primary research for Christian ministries and non-profit organizations. Since its inception in 1984, Barna Research has served several hundred parachurch ministries and thousands of churches. The firm has also served numerous non-profit clients and spent many years helping for-profit clients that have ranged from Disney, Columbia House and Southwestern Bell to Prudential, Ford, and Visa.

To date, Barna has written more than 30 books. Included among them are best-sellers such as *The Frog in the Kettle*, *The Second Coming of the Church*, *The Power of Vision*, *User Friendly Churches*, and *Marketing the Church*. His most recent books are *A Fish Out of Water* (release date: July 2002), *State of the Church: 2002* (release date: June 2002), and *Single Adults* (release date: March 2002). Several of his books have received national awards. He has also written for numerous periodicals and has published various syndicated reports on topics related to faith and lifestyle. His work is frequently cited as an authoritative source by the media.

Many people know Barna from his intensive, research-based seminars for church leaders. He is a popular speaker at ministry conferences around the world and has taught at several universities and seminaries. He has served as a pastor of a large, multi-ethnic church, has been involved in several church plants and has been on the board of directors of numerous organizations.

After graduating summa cum laude from Boston College, Barna earned two Masters degrees from Rutgers University. At Rutgers, he was awarded the Eagleton Fellowship. He also received a doctorate from Dallas Baptist University.

He lives with his wife Nancy and their two daughters (Samantha and Corban) in southern California. He enjoys spending time with his family, writing, reading, playing basketball and guitar, relaxing on the beach and visiting bookstores.

About the Barna Research Group, Ltd.

The Barna Research Group (BRG) was initiated in 1984 by George and Nancy Barna to serve the information needs of the Church. BRG's vision is "to provide Christian ministries with current, accurate and reliable information, in bite-sized pieces, at reasonable cost, to help them to be more strategic in their decision-making." The company has been honored to serve thousands of ministries since its inception.

Barna Research helps ministries by:
- offering a wealth of free, current information on-line, through the BRG web site (www.barna.org) and the bi-weekly publication of our latest findings
- conducting primary research related to specific information, development and marketing needs of an organization
- providing resources – books, reports, videos, audiotapes, newsletters – that describe BRG's research and how the findings apply to ministry

- conducting intensive seminars for church leaders, revealing insights from primary research conducted for the seminar
- presenting information in conferences, seminars and other meetings
- providing research-based consultation related to articulated ministry needs.

BRG uses both quantitative and qualitative research methods to generate relevant and reliable information that reveals insights to enhance ministry efforts. Among the types of research commonly conducted by BRG are:

- attitudinal and behavioral surveys of congregations
- lifestyle, values, behavior and beliefs profiles of communities
- profiles of the attitudes, expectations, giving habits and needs of donors
- evaluations of new products: perceived value, pricing, marketing, etc.
- name recognition and ministry image studies
- employee perception studies
- efficiency and effectiveness studies
- product use studies
- customer service and customer satisfaction
- segmentation studies to identify tapped and untapped potential
- media use surveys

If you would like to know more about Barna Research, please explore our web site. If you are interested in conducting primary research to solve some of your ministry and marketing challenges, call us at 1-800-55-BARNA. For further information, visit the Barna Research Group, Ltd. web site at www.barna.org.